MW01680666

University at Buffalo

Buffalo, New York

Written by Ben Cady

Edited by Adam Burns and Matt Hamman

Layout by Jon Skindzier

Additional contributions by Omid Gohari, Christina Koshzow, Chris Mason, Joey Rahimi, and Luke Skurman

ISBN # 1-4274-0140-3
ISSN # 1552-0714

Printed in the U.S.A.
www.collegeprowler.com

Last updated 5/19/2006

Special Thanks To: Babs Carryer, Andy Hannah, LaunchCyte, Tim O'Brien, Bob Sehlinger, Thomas Emerson, Andrew Skurman, Barbara Skurman, Bert Mann, Dave Lehman, Daniel Fayock, Chris Babyak, The Donald H. Jones Center for Entrepreneurship, Terry Slease, Jerry McGinnis, Bill Ecenberger, Idie McGinty, Kyle Russell, Jacque Zaremba, Larry Winderbaum, Roland Allen, Jon Reider, Team Evankovich, Lauren Varacalli, Abu Noaman, Mark Exler, Daniel Steinmeyer, Jared Cohon, Gabriela Oates, David Koegler, and Glen Meakem.

Bounce-Back Team: Benjamin Siegel, Jeremy J. Burton, and Jennifer Fusco.

College Prowler®
5001 Baum Blvd.
Suite 750
Pittsburgh, PA 15213

Phone: 1-800-290-2682
Fax: 1-800-772-4972
E-Mail: info@collegeprowler.com
Web Site: www.collegeprowler.com

Welcome to College Prowler®

During the writing of College Prowler's guidebooks, we felt it was critical that our content was unbiased and unaffiliated with any college or university. We think it's important that our readers get honest information and a realistic impression of the student opinions on any campus—that's why if any aspect of a particular school is terrible, we (unlike a campus brochure) intend to publish it. While we do keep an eye out for the occasional extremist—the cheerleader or the cynic—we take pride in letting the students tell it like it is. We strive to create a book that's as representative as possible of each particular campus. Our books cover both the good and the bad, and whether the survey responses point to recurring trends or a variation in opinion, these sentiments are directly and proportionally expressed through our guides.

College Prowler guidebooks are in the hands of students throughout the entire process of their creation. Because you can't make student-written guides without the students, we have students at each campus who help write, randomly survey their peers, edit, layout, and perform accuracy checks on every book that we publish. From the very beginning, student writers gather the most up-to-date stats, facts, and inside information on their colleges. They fill each section with student quotes and summarize the findings in editorial reviews. In addition, each school receives a collection of letter grades (A through F) that reflect student opinion and help to represent contentment, prominence, or satisfaction for each of our 20 specific categories. Just as in grade school, the higher the mark the more content, more prominent, or more satisfied the students are with the particular category.

Once a book is written, additional students serve as editors and check for accuracy even more extensively. Our bounce-back team—a group of randomly selected students who have no involvement with the project—are asked to read over the material in order to help ensure that the book accurately expresses every aspect of the university and its students. This same process is applied to the 200-plus schools College Prowler currently covers. Each book is the result of endless student contributions, hundreds of pages of research and writing, and countless hours of hard work. All of this has led to the creation of a student information network that stretches across the nation to every school that we cover. It's no easy accomplishment, but it's the reason that our guides are such a great resource.

When reading our books and looking at our grades, keep in mind that every college is different and that the students who make up each school are not uniform—as a result, it is important to assess schools on a case-by-case basis. Because it's impossible to summarize an entire school with a single number or description, each book provides a dialogue, not a decision, that's made up of 20 different topics and hundreds of student quotes. In the end, we hope that this guide will serve as a valuable tool in your college selection process. Enjoy!

OMID GOHARI ◯ CHRISTINA KOSHZOW ◯ CHRIS MASON ◯ JOEY RAHIMI ◯ LUKE SKURMAN ◯
The College Prowler Team

UNIVERSITY AT BUFFALO

Table of Contents

Introduction from the Author

UB is not a school for the meek. It's a big, bad state university that swaggers about its suburban plain. Coming here from high school is like moving to Manhattan from a small town—it's easy to be intimidated by the teeming masses of people and the buildings that block out the sun. But most UB students grow to love its strong academics, its truly friendly people, and the unmatched food, nightlife, and neighborhoods of Buffalo.

Two things define UB's unique culture: its size and its eclectic student body. During the week, over 27,000 students converge on two campuses for class. Over 1,600 faculty teach nearly 1,300 courses, and a total of 13 colleges offer 200 majors. And while most schools say they're diverse, no place can match UB's crazy quilt of a community—a dizzying variety of students and professors of all races, tongues, ages, classes, and talents.

UB's size means top-notch resources. But it's so big that its "institutional" aspects—lousy parking, bland campus food, and big, impersonal lower-level classes—get some people down. And while UB's diversity means life is never boring, most students say it lacks a strong campus-wide community. In sum, though nearly everyone loves their experience at UB, some students don't have nearly as much affection for the institution itself.

Once a small private school, UB became part of the State University of New York system in 1962. In a drive to become the "Berkeley of the East" (a famous cliché on campus to this day), UB brought in top faculty from all over the nation, many of whom have become legendary professors. In the '70s, most departments moved to a huge new campus in Amherst, which is the center of student life.

In recent years, the top brass has begun a push to make UB the biggest and best state university in the Northeast. Lots of money has been poured into new facilities and research centers, and with the construction of new apartments and the growth of athletics, that long-dormant campus community is slowly coming to life.

A lot of colleges strive to be small utopias, but UB is more like the real world—imperfect, but full of fascination. Most students grow to love it, both in spite of and because of its idiosyncrasies. This book will give you an honest take on what life here is really like.

Ben Cady, Author
University at Buffalo

By the Numbers

General Information

University at Buffalo
3435 Main St.
Buffalo, NY 14214

Control:
Public

Academic Calendar:
Semester

Religious Affiliation:
None

Founded:
1846

Web Site:
www.buffalo.edu

Main Phone:
(716) 645-2000

Admissions Phone:
(888) UB-ADMIT

Student Body

Full-Time Undergraduates:
16,509

Part-Time Undergraduates:
1,329

Total Male Undergraduates:
9,645

Total Female Undergraduates:
8,193

Admissions

Overall Acceptance Rate:
56%

Early Decision Acceptance Rate:
74%

Regular Acceptance Rate:
55%

Total Applicants:
18,207

Total Acceptances:
10,187

Freshman Enrollment:
3,183

Yield (% of admitted students who actually enroll):
31%

Early Decision Available?
Yes

Early Action Available?
No

Regular Decision Deadline:
February 2

Early Decision Deadline:
November 1

Early Decision Notification:
December 15

Regular Decision Deadline:
None (rolling admissions)

Regular Decision Notification:
None (rolling admissions)

Must-Reply-By Date:
May 1 (if notified after May 1, must reply within 2 weeks of notification)

Applicants Placed on Waiting List:
1,000

Applicants Accepted from Waiting List:
363

Students Enrolled from Waiting List:
97

Transfer Applications Received:
4,501

Transfer Applications Accepted:
3,037

Transfer Students Enrolled:
1,613

Transfer Application Acceptance Rate:
67%

Common Application Accepted?
No

Supplemental Forms?
No

Admissions E-Mail:
ub-admissions@buffalo.edu

Admissions Web Site:
www.buffalo.edu/admissions

➜

SAT I or ACT Required?
Either SAT or ACT required

SAT I Range (25th–75th Percentile):
1070–1250

SAT I Verbal Range (25th–75th Percentile):
520–610

SAT I Math Range (25th–75th Percentile):
550–640

Retention Rate:
85%

Top 10% of High School Class:
24%

Application Fee:
$40

Financial Information

In-State Tuition:
$6,070

Out-of-State Tuition:
$13,330

Room and Board:
$7,226

Books and Supplies:
$750

Average Need-Based Financial Aid Package:
$7,132

Students Who Applied for Financial Aid:
73%

Students Who Received Aid:
54%

Financial Aid Forms Deadline:
March 1

Financial Aid Phone:
(716) 645-2450 or
1-866-838-7257

Financial Aid E-Mail:
srcenter@buffalo.edu

Financial Aid Web Site:
http://src.buffalo.edu

Academics

The Lowdown On... Academics

Degrees Awarded:

Associate
Bachelor
Master
Post-Master Certificate
First Professional
Doctorate

Most Popular Majors:

18% Business
13% Social Sciences
11% Engineering
10% Communications
9% Psychology

Undergraduate Schools:

College of Arts and Sciences
School of Architecture and Planning
School of Engineering and Applied Sciences
School of Informatics
School of Management
School of Pharmacy and Pharmaceutical Sciences

Full-Time Faculty:

1,121

→

Faculty with Terminal Degree:
98%

Student-to-Faculty Ratio:
15:1

Graduation Rates:
Four-Year: 34%
Five-Year: 53%
Six-Year: 60%

Best Places to Study

Charles B. Sears Law Library, Health Sciences Library, Lockwood Memorial Library

Combined Degree Programs

Chemical Engineering/Business Administration BS/MBA
Civil Engineering/Business Administration BS/MBA
Computational Physics/Physics BS/MS
Computer Science/Business Administration BA/MBA
Economics/Business Administration BA/MBA
Electrical Engineering/Business Administration BS/MBA
Exercise Science/Nutrition BS/MS
Industrial Engineering/Business Administration BS/MBA
Joint Aerospace Engineering/Business BS/MBA
Mechanical Engineering/Business BS/MBA
Social Sciences Interdisciplinary/Social Work BA/MSW
Sociology/Business Administration BA/MBA

Sample Academic Clubs

Association for Computing Machinery, Art Historical Association, Minority Management Club, Nursing Student Organization, Political Science Student Association, Pre-Law Society, Writers Association

AP Test Score Requirements

Possible credit for scores of 3, 4, and 5

IB Test Score Requirements

Possible credit for scores of 5, 6, and 7

Did You Know?

? UB offers **more academic programs** than any other public university in New York State or New England.

Professors and students play a major role in Buffalo's cutting-edge arts community. UB will soon **host the largest exhibition** of contemporary Chinese art in the history of the United States.

Giant shake tables at the Multidisciplinary Center for Earthquake Engineering Research **simulate earthquakes** and allow engineers to study how to build structures along faults. The shake tables are the largest and most advanced in the world.

The Poetry and Rare Books Library in Capen Hall has **extensive collections of original manuscripts** by James Joyce, William Carlos Williams, and Robert Graves, including the original drafts and manuscripts of Joyce's *Ulysses* and *Finnegan's Wake*. The original manuscript of Twain's *Huckleberry Finn* is housed in the Buffalo Central Library.

The November 2003 edition of *Scientific American* named Thomas Szyperski, a professor in the department of chemistry, among its "**Scientific American 50**," a list of the world's 50 most accomplished researchers.

UB's English department **is one of the nation's best**. When the 2001 edition of the *Norton Anthology of Contemporary Poetry* was published, four of the poets in the anthology were UB professors. The following year, a UB English professor was awarded the Pulitzer Prize for poetry. In 2003, eminent professor and literary critic Leslie Fiedler—who some credit with applying the concepts of postmodernism to literature—died after 40 years as a UB professor.

Students Speak Out On... Academics

"The academics are decent depending on the department. However, the huge selection of classes in almost any subject area you can think of is great."

"The **academics here are all over the place**. I've had teachers to whom I never spoke one-on-one, simply because there were so many students in the class. But I've also gotten to know a couple of my teachers personally. There's an abundance of international TAs, which can be cool, but there's often an inhibiting language barrier."

"The academics, like most things at any college, are what you make of them. **Gen ed requirements are a pain**—especially freshman year—but there's not much you can do except get them out of the way ASAP, and even then, they're not that bad."

"**Freshmen are herded into the lecture halls like cattle to the meat grinder**. The powers that be shove up to 400 kids in a class, mostly taught by TAs, while at the same time, glorifying the University for its renowned faculty. After freshman year, though, the classes thin out; now that I'm a senior, most of my classes are 20 kids, and they're taught by the professors that the recruitment brochures had touted so highly."

"**The fine arts programs are worth every penny**, as are the humanities-related departments. I know many people who have gone to UB for an English degree, and they all say they've gotten a great education."

"**You get a huge mix of intelligence from the students**. I got a 1080 on my SATs, and I have class with kids that scored over 1400. That doesn't mean you can't do well—sometimes they don't work hard in class, and you have a chance to topple them."

"The classes and teachers here are among the best. You get a variety of teachers with different styles which add more jazz to the classes. Sure, there are **some boring teachers and classes**, but that's expected. They even offer a class called The Dinosaurs."

"Notwithstanding the very large student body, the large lecture classes are too big. With so many departments, it's obvious **the departments have to funnel their resources into large classes**, but it often becomes detrimental to our education. There has got to be other ways to teach students other than in large masses."

"There is always a wide variety of courses offered in each department, and they change frequently from semester to semester. They have **some really unique and fun classes**, such as a *Lord of the Rings* class and a tourism planning class."

"Academics at UB are pretty good. There are many different classes, **from higher-level mathematics to racquetball**. The student body is usually pretty good at letting you know who the bad teachers are, so make friends with a few upperclassmen in your major!"

"Most students are friendly. However, in my pre-med classes, there were many students who were very competitive in class. There is also **always one annoying student in each large lecture class** who tries to act smart by asking too many questions with as many big words as possible. Do not be intimidated, as these students are often the worst in the class."

"Academics have an extreme range of difficulty and depth. There are plenty of classes to take here, and for those who are obsessed with knowledge, you may never leave. Some classes are in giant lecture halls, and **it is easy to feel lost**; however, I find it more enjoyable, because I enjoy searching through the crowds of people and finding the best spot to hunt for the females in the class."

"Class sizes decrease in upper-level classes, and professors are more personal. I've never had a professor who did not promptly respond to an e-mail. **Take advantage of technology**, and e-mail professors questions if you can't make it to their office hours."

"My departments of expertise are the business, art, and media departments. **The business department generally has been very good**; I have only had a few bad teachers. The good thing about this department is that many of the teachers work in the field they are teaching, so they are very wise about the real-world situation."

"Foreign-born TAs in intro classes are often hard to learn anything from. **Every once in a while, a good TA is found**. Take advantage of this—ask questions and develop a friendly relationship."

"**The academics at UB are fine**. Some classes are really tough; others are criminally easy. Though many of the school's program administrations are incompetent (the business school, for example), if you follow the rules, you'll do fine."

The College Prowler Take On... Academics

There's a small bunch of highly intellectual students who frequent office hours, take graduate classes, get involved in research, and sprint for fellowships and Phi Beta Kappa keys. At first, these kids are often frustrated by the lack of intellectual energy at UB, but most seek it out in small classes, academic clubs, or professors' homes. Then there's everybody else: students who care about their grades and want to get a good job after college, but keep quiet in class and steer clear of the library until finals week. These students (many of whom are paying their own way) are generally happy with their UB education, but they often gripe about big classes and boring TAs.

The academic scene, like so much else at UB, lives and dies by the school's size. UB is one of the most productive research universities in the nation. Students have an extraordinary variety of things to study. Many build their own majors, join a five-year program, or switch majors one, two, or three times. Most of its schools are ranked well nationally, and some, such as the business and engineering schools, are ranked among the best in the world. Professors are popular and accessible. Come registration time, the choice of classes is nearly infinite. But the school's size can be an obstacle. While most students like their professors, most dislike big lecture classes, especially if they are taught by TAs. Few students forget the first time they put their ID number at the top of a test instead of their name. Undergraduate study also shares the limelight with the mostly top-flight graduate schools and the research culture. Some of UB's harshest critics say the school is nothing but a "research university." But even those students who feel alienated by UB's size generally agree that you can't beat it for the price.

B

The College Prowler® Grade on

Academics: B

A high Academics grade generally indicates that professors are knowledgeable, accessible, and genuinely interested in their students' welfare. Other determining factors include class size, how well professors communicate, and whether or not classes are engaging.

Local Atmosphere

The Lowdown On... Local Atmosphere

Region:
Northeast

City, State:
Buffalo, NY

Setting:
City

Distance from Niagara Falls:
30 minutes

Distance from Toronto:
90 minutes

Distance from New York:
7 hours

Distance from Boston:
7 hours

➜

Points of Interest:

Albright-Knox Art Gallery

Buffalo Historical Society

Buffalo Zoo

Casino Niagara

Darwin D. Martin House

Elmwood Village

Hallwalls Contemporary Art Center

HSBC Arena

Kleinhans Music Hall

Niagara Falls

Our Lady of Victory Basilica

Ralph Wilson Stadium

Shea's Performing Arts Center

Theodore Roosevelt Inaugural Site at the Wilcox Mansion

Closest Shopping Malls or Plazas:

Boulevard Mall

Walden Galleria

Closest Movie Theaters:

Dipson Amherst Theater
3500 Main St., University Heights
(716) 834-7655

Maple Ridge 8
4276 Maple Rd. (at Sweet Home Rd.), Amherst
(716) 833-9545

North Park Theater
1428 Hertel Ave., Buffalo
(716) 836-7411

Major Sports Teams:

Buffalo Bills (NFL football)

Buffalo Bisons (Triple-A baseball, International League)

Buffalo Sabres (NHL hockey)

City Web Sites

www.buffalo.com

www.city-buffalo.com

Did You Know?

5 Fun Facts about Buffalo:

- Buffalo has one of the nation's most vibrant art scenes. Albright-Knox Art Gallery boasts one of the **best collections of modern art** in the world, including major paintings and sculptures by artists from Picasso to Warhol. *American Style* magazine has consistently ranked Buffalo among the top 10 American cities for the arts.
- Many of the most important American architects, including Stanford White, H.H. Richardson, Louis Sullivan, Frank Lloyd Wright, Eero Saarinen, Gordon Bunshaft, and Max Abramovitz, **have major buildings in Buffalo**.
- At its heart, Buffalo **is an industrial city**. The first concrete grain elevator was built along the Buffalo River, and the first supersonic aircraft was built at the Curtiss-Wright factory on Elmwood Avenue. Today, because of its proximity to Canada, Buffalo is ranked among the United States' 10 most important cities for international commerce.
- While Buffalo has suffered through many epic blizzards, including a week-long storm in 2001 that dumped 12 feet of snow on the city, **the average annual snowfall is lower than Rochester and Syracuse**. Buffalo has a higher percentage of summer sunshine than any Northeast city.
- Niagara Falls, **one of the world's most popular tourist destinations** and a favorite nightlife destination for UB students, is located within the Buffalo metropolitan area—about 30 minutes from campus.

Famous Buffalonians:

Harold Arlen (Broadway composer)

Lucille Ball (actress)

Wolf Blitzer (CNN anchor)

Samuel Clemens (author also known as Mark Twain)

Grover Cleveland (U.S. president)

Ani DiFranco (recording artist)

Former President Millard Fillmore

Rick James (funk singer)

→

(Famous Buffalonians, continued)

Milton Rogovin (famous photographer)

Mark Russell (political satirist)

Tim Russert (host of *Meet the Press*)

Johnny Rzeznik (lead singer of the Goo Goo Dolls)

Warren Spahn (Hall of Fame pitcher)

Martha Stewart (former host of *Martha Stewart Living*)

Grover Washington Jr. (jazz composer)

Local Slang:

Blue – Labatt Blue.

Dere/Dah/Dat – "There," "the," and "that" in the famous Buffalo accent, much like the Chicago accent in the old "Da Bears" skit on *Saturday Night Live*.

GST – Goods and services tax, charged on items bought in Canada.

The Heights – The run-down but well-loved student neighborhood around South Campus.

The Main Line – What locals call Interstate 90 (the New York State Thruway) as it passes through town.

The Northtowns – The northern suburbs, including Amherst, where North Campus is located.

The Queen City – Buffalo's most popular nickname, which has a double meaning because of the city's close-knit and visible gay community.

Pop – What Buffalo residents call soda (and New York City natives find themselves using grudgingly after four years at UB).

The Southtowns – The southern suburbs and small towns, including Orchard Park (where the Bills play) and Ellicottville (where the ski resorts are).

Weck – A kimmelweck roll, on which Buffalo's famous hot roast beef sandwiches are served.

You'se – What old people around Buffalo say instead of "you" (as in "You'se college kids over dere better keep dat racket down!").

Students Speak Out On... Local Atmosphere

"The Amherst atmosphere is completely harmless and completely boring. It's better to be living close to the bars on Main Street and the much better bars on Elmwood."

"Amherst itself doesn't really have a college town atmosphere. **South Campus and downtown Buffalo are pretty cool**. There's usually something to do, but a car (or a friend with a car) is nice to have. The campus really grows on you."

"The area is terrific if you're into art and music. **There are great scenes for hardcore and jam band aficionados**. Also, while not as many popular acts stop here as in Toronto and New York, Buffalo is one of the mainstay stops for most traveling bands."

"**There's something for everyone in Buffalo**. Once in downtown, there's a gallery, theater, or movie house every few blocks. Buffalo boasts one of the most thriving art scenes in the state, from contemporary art to photography to sculpture and back again. The problem, it seems, is getting students to venture from the comfort of their dorms in Amherst into the city. While a subway system connects South Campus to downtown, few students utilize it."

"**Atmosphere makes Buffalo**. From eateries to bars to Canada, there is always something to do here."

"There are things to do. Movies, food, Lasertron, malls. **It's not the sticks**."

"The atmosphere in Buffalo is one of the most depressing atmospheres in existence. **The city is economically crippled**, and the entire Main Street stretch between Broadway Joe's (at the end of University Heights) to Shea's Performing Arts Center (at the beginning of downtown) looks like the run-down parts of Queens."

"The atmosphere in Amherst is **perfect for college kids looking to escape school**. When you travel down Amherst's roads, you see malls and well-developed commercial parks full of Fuddruckers, Tully's Sports Bars, Hooters, bowling alleys, and Krispy Kreme doughnuts joints."

"I have lived on campus for all four years, which I like, but it is **very difficult to get off campus without a car** because the North Campus is isolated just farther than walking distance from almost anywhere. At first glance, it seems like the city of Buffalo has nothing to do, but if you ask the students who grew up in the area, they will offer many suggestions of Buffalo's hidden treasures."

"Being situated right next to an international border is a definite plus. It takes about as long to get to Canada as it does to downtown Buffalo, and **the drinking age is 19**, and you can look at Niagara Falls."

"As far as Amherst goes, there are tons of places to eat, spend your money, see movies, and experience **the middle- to upper-class suburbs**. But you need a car, so many of Williamsville and Amherst's streets are practically highways. A bike would be better than not having a car, but it certainly wouldn't be without leg cramps."

"There's a lot of fun stuff to do, including **Sabres hockey and indie-rock shows**. The Bills play 30 minutes from campus in Orchard Park."

The College Prowler Take On...
Local Atmosphere

Depending on the student, "Buffalo" means one of three very different parts of town. There's Amherst, a bland, pancake-flat, upper-middle-class suburb within which North Campus is itself isolated by rings of fields and highways. There's the Heights, a vibrant area around South Campus chock full of bars and shops where students pack into big brick houses and bursting bungalows. And there's the rest of Buffalo, equal parts decaying industrial city and friendly, liberal college town, where many students party, study, and make their homes.

Most students are immediately bored by Amherst. It is peaceful, safe, and even verdant in the fall (before winter comes and dirty piles of plowed snow line its highways), but after a few months, students realize there's not much to do other than run on the bike path or drive to Duff's and Denny's. The Heights has a completely different atmosphere—it's the Mick Jagger to Amherst's Clay Aiken. There are bars, diners, ethnic restaurants, stores, and coffee shops, and at night, you can walk from parties to bars. But the extent to which students enjoy UB often depends on how well they get to know the "real" Buffalo. From South Campus, the city stretches west to the Niagara River and south to Lake Erie. It's a shabby, friendly, and surprisingly sophisticated town. Buffalo has a dynamic arts community, excellent museums, a fine orchestra, and the beloved Bills and Sabres, whose games most students go to see at least once. The cost of living is less than half of what it is in larger cities. And with the bars open until 4 a.m. and Niagara Falls, Canada just miles away, many students find atmosphere to be Buffalo's best quality.

B+

The College Prowler® Grade on

Local Atmosphere: B+

A high Local Atmosphere grade indicates that the area surrounding campus is safe and scenic. Other factors include nearby attractions, proximity to other schools, and the town's attitude toward students.

Safety & Security

The Lowdown On... Safety & Security

Number of UB Police:
60

UB Police Phone:
(716) 645-2222

Health Center Office Hours:
Monday 9 a.m.–7 p.m.,
Tuesday–Friday 9 a.m.–5 p.m.,
Saturday 9 a.m.–3 p.m.

Safety Services:
- Criminal investigation
- Crime prevention and community policing
- Door locking and Night Host programs
- Emergency response
- Operation Identification/ Book ID
- Project Kidcare
- Safety escorts
- Self-defense workshops
- Women's safety and sexual assault prevention programs

→

→

Health Services:

Allergy shots
Basic medical services
Counseling services
Dental care
Dietitian
Immunizations
Infectious disease clinic
Travel clinic
Weight clinic
Women's health clinic

Did You Know?

?

In 2003, Amherst was named **America's safest city** by the Quitno Institute, an independent research company that analyzes crime rates. Amherst, the home of North Campus, has won the award in five of the past eight years.

Students Speak Out On... Safety & Security

"There is a moderate amount of crime in the University Heights area, though I have never heard of any major, serious crimes being committed on the dorms or on North Campus."

"North Campus is nestled in the Amherst community, which has consistently been ranked the safest town in America. Makes you feel safe, right? The only problem with this fact is that UB's crime stats are not included in the rankings. Crime at UB, while tame compared to some universities, exists. On Easter, my CD player was stolen from my car while I was at church. **I've had my mirror on my car stolen twice**."

"North Campus is fairly safe, but **South Campus is more urban and has a greater amount of crime**. It's not uncommon to hear about an occasional car break-in or vandalism in University Heights. Walking around University Heights is fairly safe, but it is usually a good idea to walk with someone else. I've also heard the health care at Michael Hall leaves something to be desired."

"South Campus lies at the edge of Buffalo's Eastside, an area known for its crime and drug problems. I live in University Heights, an area near South Campus. Last year, **all the cars in my driveway were broken into**; all the valuables from each car were stolen. The lesson I learned is that crime happens everywhere. The area is far from the ghetto, but don't be stupid. Don't walk alone, whether in Amherst or Detroit or New York City or Pleasantville."

"The safety issue is odd. While I've never had anything happen to me, I've heard about **a lot of crime on and around campus**. Things I never would have encountered in my hometown are serious threats here."

"I'm as paranoid as they come, and I feel pretty safe on this campus. But keep the 4 a.m. jogs at a minimum—maybe not at all. **Crime is minimal, except for those bouts of abductions and a few robberies** here and there. Health facilities are suitable, as well. Once, I thought I was dying of meningitis and I had an officer at my door in about five minutes. So emergency health services gets a thumbs-up."

"I have yet to use Michael Hall, the student health center, since my arrival at UB. But, as an RA last year, I had to call the campus police on a few occasions. They were always **prompt and helpful**."

"Everywhere on North Campus is relatively safe. South Campus is a different story. My brother lived there for a semester, and every night at varying times, he heard police sirens. One of his roommates got jumped for all his money while walking down Main Street, and when the people who jumped him found out he only had a few bucks on him, they **pistol-whipped him in the face**. I just don't think I'd walk around South Campus at night after hearing that."

"As a student Public Safety aide, I can assure you there is plenty of protection for the students. There is the occasional crime, usually theft, but since I've been here **I have yet to see a fight break out**—far different from high school. Pretty much the only crimes I've seen are damage of public or private property."

"The fact that the campus is divided in two, I believe, makes it a safer environment. Being on a smaller campus, there is not as far to go to get where you need. The campus has a great bus system that circles the campus and drops you off pretty close to wherever you need to be. The parking lots are also lit pretty well. Personally, **I have never felt scared or in danger** walking to my car after a night class, and I've had one every semester of my college career."

"Robbery of stereos from cars is common on South Campus. **You can't really have anything nice around here**."

The College Prowler Take On...
Safety & Security

Surveying the campus police blotter in Wednesday's issue of the *Spectrum* is a popular ritual at UB because most of the crimes are harmless—a stolen laser pointer from the natural sciences building, a case of indigestion in one of the dining halls, a false fire alarm in a dormitory, and now and then, students caught having sex in a dark classroom. North Campus is nestled in a suburban town that has been named the safest in the U.S., but while students have a reason and a right to feel safe, UB is not without its odd quality-of-life crimes. Often these crimes can be chalked up to students who don't take precautions: the laptop stolen from the unlocked room, the clothes taken from the unattended dryer, the stereo yanked from the car parked with its windows down. By junior or senior year, most students know someone who has been a victim. If you're coming from a rural area or a small town, you should read some public safety pamphlets in the first few weeks of school to learn how to avoid minor crimes.

Security is a more serious issue on South Campus and in University Heights. During the day, students and faculty can be confident in their safety, but at night, neither men nor women should walk anywhere alone, and students should steer clear of areas that are particularly dark or empty. Burglaries can happen if doors are not locked, and rarely, but sometimes, more serious crimes occur. Luckily, students who do not feel comfortable living with the uncertainties of an urban environment can stay on North Campus, which—save for the odd quality-of-life crime—is as secure as a castle with a moat.

C

The College Prowler® Grade on

Safety & Security: C

A high grade in Safety & Security means that students generally feel safe, campus police are visible, blue-light phones and escort services are readily available, and safety precautions are not overly necessary.

Computers

The Lowdown On... Computers

High-Speed Network?
Yes

Wireless Network?
Yes

Number of Labs:
7

Number of Computers:
About 1,800 in campus labs

Operating Systems:
Linux, Mac OS, Unix, Windows

Discounted Software

UB Micro, the non-profit on-campus computer store, sells software at market price.

Free Software

Ad-Aware, Adobe Acrobat Reader, AIM Express, Aladdin Expander, EndNote, Internet Explorer, Microsoft Office, Mulberry, Netscape, Norton Anti-Virus, QuickTime, Real Player, Shockwave, SSH Secure Shell, UBFS Home, UBiquity Citrix Environment, UBVPN, WS_FTP, X-Win 32

24-Hour Labs

Undergraduate Library (Microsoft), 101 Bell Hall (Unix/Linux)

Charge to Print?

No

Did You Know?

The Dell Cluster at the Center for Computational Research in Norton Hall is **one of the world's 10 largest supercomputers**, and the fourth fastest academic supercomputer in the world.

Yahoo! Internet Life magazine ranked UB one of the nation's top 10 "**Most Wired Universities**" in 2001.

About **75 million sheets of paper** are printed annually in the campus libraries, where printing is free.

Students Speak Out On...
Computers

"There are a couple of lesser-known labs, and if you can find one of these, you can generally get a computer and print out your stuff relatively quickly."

"The network is an incredible tool. It's **one of the fastest connections on the East Coast**. The labs do get very busy in the first weeks and last weeks of the semester, but for the most part a seat can be found, unless you're looking on the first floor of Capen."

"As long as you're smart about when you use the computer labs, **you shouldn't have a problem without a computer**. There are so many computer labs on campus that it's just a matter of figuring out when certain ones are busy. Planning ahead helps. Going to the Capen lab five minutes before your term paper's due won't work too well."

"My freshman year, they updated from T3 to OC-3. The LAN on campus, in the dorms, was upgraded from 10 MBps to 100 MBps. All on-campus apartments are also wired at 100 MBps. Now, **download speeds from the Internet average about 1.5 MB/second**."

"**Computer labs are always crowded**, but there are also many more portals available that students don't even know exist. I would say that if they were more adequately promoted, we'd all be waiting in shorter lines and a whole lot happier. The printing cue line is really atrocious, though."

"I don't have a computer, so I use the computer labs. They are free, there is no time limit, and the copies are free. But **it can get crowded near the end of the semester**, and the printing wait is always over an hour. It's better than buying a computer, though!"

"The Unix machines for engineers are supplied by Sun Microsystems. **They are powerful machines**, but if a lot of people are in the lab the day before something is due, the server gets bogged down. Recently, half of the main Unix lab was replaced by Dell machines, running the newest version of Redhat Linux written specifically for UB. For programming, these machines are a good amount faster than the Sun machines, but other things the Sun machines were good for have not been completely debugged on the Linux machines. Hopefully these problems will be rectified over the summer."

"During the last two years, wireless has become ubiquitous on campus. People eat lunch at the Student Union or at Bert's while instant messaging their friends or putting the finishing touches on a project due during their next class. **The wireless access isn't as fast as the latest wireless standard**, and it varies based on how far the machines are from the access point, but it's sufficient for most applications."

"UB offers one of the best computer networks in the country, hands down. There are thousands of computers available on campus for students, and there are many free programs for students, such as Microsoft Office. **UB also has a supercomputer** that is ranked as one of the fastest in the world. One place to stay away from is UB Micro, the on-campus computer store. They claim to be non-profit, but the prices are ridiculous, and the service is unfriendly."

"The computer labs can be a little frustrating if you don't know how to time them right. First, you need to understand that a lot of teachers are really **good at making notes, and sometimes texts, available online**. Second, you need to know that UB offers free printing. So now, you can imagine a lecture of 300 students, each trying to print up to 100 pages of notes—it's craziness. There are sometimes up to 24-hour delays in the printouts. Once your stuff is printed, however, the print desk hangs onto it for 24 hours."

"The computer network is amazing! The help desk service is always on top of things. **Downloading is done at lighting-fast speeds**. The computer labs are never full—at least from what I have seen—but I would bring my own PC, just to avoid going outside in the cold!"

"There are **a ton of computer labs all over campus**, including a lab in the dorms. You should still definitely bring your own computer because, while you can almost always get one, the printing lines are becoming almost ridiculous."

"In the dorms, **UB offers the fastest network my computer has ever seen**. The computer labs are hardly ever full or crowded. I feel that having your own computer is a necessity wherever you go, but at UB, you could definitely get away without one. To most college students, their computers are basically the ADD machine, complete with AOL Instant Messenger."

"**UB students are online all the time**. Bring a desktop, because laptops have a tendency to get stolen or misplaced. Fast connections all over campus provide instant access and printing facilities, so you don't have to spend money on ink or paper. I haven't paid for ink since freshman year."

The College Prowler Take On...
Computers

Everybody is impressed with UB's powerful computer network, from researchers mapping the human genome to dorm residents downloading *Old School* and *Van Wilder*. There are nearly 2,000 public site computers on campus in dozens of labs. A growing wireless network covers most of the campus. Almost every classroom has a fancy teaching station with a computer and projector. And the fourth fastest academic supercomputer in the world sits behind thick glass windows (and a fingerprint-identification lock) on the first floor of Norton Hall.

Students are generally pleased with UB's computer labs, called "cybraries." Many students (particularly international students) don't bring their own computers and use the cybraries full time. Still, many students who have their own computers use the cybraries because printing is free. As a result, the most popular cybraries are crowded during peak hours (wait times can reach 15–20 minutes). And in the beginning of the semester when students print their lecture notes, print queues can be as long as five to ten hours, though waits go down to fifteen minutes to an hour by the middle of the semester. Computers are also slowly entering UB's academic culture, as well. Some professors post course notes and information on a site called "UB Learns," and each year, more and more professors use listservs for class discussion, sometimes offering extra credit for students who post.

A

The College Prowler® Grade on

Computers: A

A high grade in Computers designates that computer labs are available, the computer network is easily accessible, and the campus' computing technology is up-to-date.

Facilities

The Lowdown On... Facilities

Student Center:
The Student Union, North Campus; Harriman Hall, South Campus

Athletic Centers:
Alumni Arena (North Campus); Clark Hall (South Campus)

Libraries:
10

Popular Places to Chill:
Alumni, Baird Point, Bert's, the Commons (especially Campus Café and Starbucks), the Ellicott Bowl, the Undergraduate Library (where the no-talking rules are never enforced), and the Union on North Campus; Clark, Harriman, the Hayes lawn, and the Squire Quad on South Campus

Campus Size:
1,350 acres

What Is There to Do on Campus?

Several options for PG-rated fun are available in the big and bustling Student Union at the center of campus. Here, you can catch a nap in the Commuter Lounge, battle it out with a friend over a Ping-Pong or pool table, test drive a massage chair in the Wellness Center, or get some eats in Putnam's or Pistachio's. Alumni Arena is close enough to the academic buildings that many students work out between classes. The Center for the Arts hosts daily cultural events and houses an excellent art gallery.

Movie Theater on Campus?

Not officially, but discounted movies are often shown in the Student Union theater.

Bowling on Campus?

No

Bar on Campus?

No

Coffeehouse on Campus?

Yes—Starbucks, the Commons; Perks, Ellicott Food Court

Favorite Things to Do

Frats and sororities send their pledges up to campus in the early morning hours to stake out prime Student Union tables, which their brothers and sisters then keep all day. Though most students can't handle that grueling schedule, the Student Union is the most popular place for students on campus to relax. The bright, lively lobby is a great place to watch the influx and efflux of people. On any given night, a handful of UB's 200 student organizations is doing something interesting on campus—often in the Union's theater, social hall, or flag room. The Center for the Arts hosts many touring concerts and plays, in addition to productions by theater and dance majors or music students. During the winter and spring, students go to basketball games and play IM sports at Alumni Arena.

Students Speak Out On... Facilities

"UB's facilities are great. There are many libraries. Most large lecture halls have large video projectors that can show PowerPoint slides or videos."

"Facilities on North Campus are pretty modern, and they offer you the luxury of walking inside through the academic buildings **without having to go outside** for the 10 months of the year when it's freezing."

"In general, the facilities on campus are fine. Alumni Arena is a perfect place to work out, play some basketball, or swim in an Olympic-size swimming pool. Aside from Alumni, the rest of the campus **isn't exactly eye-candy**. The academic buildings and dorms serve their respective purposes, but nobody really went for broke when designing them."

"The Student Union houses all of the clubs and student governments, the Office of Student Life, and the newspaper and magazine. In addition, it's one of the **finest sources of non-nutritious meals** on campus—Putnam's. It's the hub of the campus, and it's impossible to pass through without running into that guy from your stats class or the girl you met at last week's party. With music usually blasting through the building and hordes of people eating lunch and dinner, the Union is one of the most integral, and most fun, places on campus."

"The Student Union leaves **much to be desired**. It's a big open atrium that's never quite clean with bad food and poor acoustics. Fortunately, there are nicer places to visit and eat on campus. Lockwood Library makes a fantastic study place with its big round windows and low-level lighting. And it's pleasant to watch dancers or robots or painters while you snack and study in the Center for the Arts atrium."

"The Student Union is nice; however, I almost never use it. The athletic facilities are also nice, depending on what you need to use them for. Unfortunately, UB does not have a decent indoor track facility at all. All they have is the 'jogging track' in Alumni Arena, which **tends to be hot and overcrowded**. The Commons has a large selection of stores, but because I live off campus, I have no use for them."

"The facilities at UB are **either very nice or simply adequate**. The sports facilities are big and exciting, and the Student Union is always bustling with activity. There are a lot of interesting places off the beaten path, such as the comfy Commuter Lounge, where you can catch a snooze right after your 8 a.m. class."

"The workout facilities are poor. There are lines to get on every machine, and the equipment is old. The whole look and atmosphere of the weight room is dark and gloomy. There is no music and no place to put clothes taken off during a workout. The locker rooms aren't very pleasant either. I can't speak for the women's locker room, but the men's locker room is very beat up, and it looks like it **hasn't been renovated in 20 years**. Naked old men make frequent appearances everywhere."

"**The facilities all have a different feel to them**. The entire classroom area on North Campus is all connected, so you don't ever have to go outside to get to a class in the winter. The Union is sort of like a party, where everybody meets to hang out or study. Everything is state-of-the-art."

"The on-campus facilities have everything I could ask. The Student Union has its own movie theater, where films are shown on a weekly basis. The gyms are pretty decent. Alumni Arena has a great selection of free weights and aerobic machines. It also can be **used for martial-arts classes**—that's where I get my ju jutsu practice."

"The facilities are real nice. However, **public bathrooms are shady at best**. Some rooms smell for no reason."

"The facilities on campus are all up-to-date and well maintained. All the buildings on North Campus are **connected through tunnels and bridges**, which is very useful on the winter walks to class. I have no problem with any of the complexes."

The College Prowler Take On...
Facilities

Most students who come to UB hate the way North Campus looks at first; it's built not like a traditional college, but like a '70s vision of a "college of the future." In time, though, nearly everyone gets used to the campus, and many grow to like it. South Campus has a more traditional feel. Its ivy-covered facilities are weathered and worn by the years, but its scenic quads and sloping lawns are beautiful. Students give North Campus high marks for the tunnels and bridges that connect all the buildings along the "Spine" (the cluster of academic buildings at the center of campus). It's possible to take off your coat in the winter and go to all your classes without braving the cold. Most students' favorite building on campus is the noisy, crowded Student Union, which is the scene of so many of the serendipitous encounters that make college life memorable. Harriman Hall, which has been a student union since the 1920s, is a popular gathering place for the South Campus crowd. Artsy architecture majors and med students in light blue scrubs gather for lunch in high-ceilinged rooms with chandeliers.

UB's libraries get high marks for their deep collections and friendly staff, but some are better places to study than others. Students praise Lockwood for its big study areas and austere, modern atmosphere. Older students find the Undergraduate Library (more appropriately called the "Freshman Library") to be loud and ugly. The dorm complexes on both campuses are so big that they have their own computer labs, study areas, and workout rooms. In terms of quality of life, the two campuses are nearly opposite experiences. Students on North overcome their dislike for the campus's aesthetics because of its high-quality facilities, while students on South tolerate the worn-out facilities because of the campus's charm.

A-

The College Prowler® Grade on

Facilities: A-

A high Facilities grade indicates that the campus is aesthetically pleasing and well-maintained; facilities are state-of-the-art, and libraries are exceptional. Other determining factors include the quality of both athletic and student centers and an abundance of things to do on campus.

Campus Dining

The Lowdown On... Campus Dining

Freshman Meal Plan Requirement?

Yes, for those who live on campus

Meal Plan Average Cost:

$1,075–$1,815 per semester

Places to Grab a Bite with Your Meal Plan:

Baldy Walkway Café

Food: Sandwiches, snacks

Location: Baldy Hall

Hours: Monday–Friday 8 a.m.–2 p.m.

Bert's

Food: Breakfast, Mexican, salads, pizza, Starbucks

Location: Talbert Hall, North Campus

Hours: Monday–Friday 7:30 a.m.–2:30 p.m.

→

Bert's Kosher Deli

Food: Kosher

Location: Talbert Hall, North Campus

Hours: Monday–Friday 11 a.m.–2 p.m.

Capen Café

Food: Salads, sandwiches, fruit, pizza

Location: Capen Hall, North Campus

Hours: Monday 8 a.m.–6 p.m., Tuesday 8 a.m.–7 p.m., Wednesday 8 a.m.–6 p.m., Thursday 8 a.m.–7 p.m., Friday 8 a.m.–4 p.m.

The Cellar

Food: American grill, Mexican

Location: Governors Hall, North Campus

Hours: Monday–Friday 11 a.m.–1:30 p.m., 7 p.m.–11:30 p.m., Saturday 7:30 p.m.–11:30 p.m., Sunday 7 p.m.–12 a.m.

Center for the Arts Café (CFA Café)

Food: Unique soups and sandwiches

Location: Center for the Arts, North Campus

Hours: Monday–Thursday 8:30 a.m.–5 p.m., Friday 8:30 a.m.–1:30 p.m.

Farber Café

Food: Lunch bar

Location: Farber Hall, South Campus

Hours: Monday–Friday 8:30 a.m.–1:30 p.m.

Governors Dining Center

Food: All-you-can-eat, cafeteria-style

Location: Governors Hall

Hours: Monday–Friday 7 a.m.–10 a.m., 4:30 p.m.–6:30 p.m., Saturday–Sunday 11 a.m.–1:30 p.m., 4:30 p.m.–6:30 p.m.

The Greenery

Food: Full-service restaurant

Location: Harriman Hall, South Campus

Hours: Monday–Friday 11:30 a.m.–1:30 p.m.

Greens and Beans

Food: Soups and salads

Location: Ellicott Complex, North Campus

Hours: Monday–Friday 11 a.m.–7 p.m.

Harriman Café

Food: Pizza, subs, salads, grill

Location: Harriman Hall, South Campus

Hours: Monday–Friday 7 a.m.–2 p.m.

Hubies

Food: Pizza, subs, salads, grill

Location: Ellicott Complex, North Campus

Hours: Monday–Thursday 11 a.m.–12 a.m., Friday 11 a.m.–11 p.m., Saturday 5 p.m.–11 p.m., Sunday 5 p.m.–12 a.m.

Perks

Food: Coffee shop with desserts and ice cream

Location: Ellicott Complex, North Campus

Hours: Monday–Thursday 8 a.m.–12 a.m., Friday 8 a.m.–9 p.m., Saturday 10 a.m.–9 p.m., Sunday 10 a.m.–12 a.m.

Pistachio's

Food: Upscale deli

Location: Student Union, North Campus

Hours: Monday–Friday 11 a.m.–2 p.m.

Putnam's

Food: Deli, tacos, pizza, sushi

Location: Student Union, North Campus

Hours: Monday–Friday 8 a.m.–7:30 p.m.

Red Jacket Dining Center

Food: All-you-can-eat, cafeteria-style

Location: Ellicott Complex, North Campus

(Red Jacket Dining Center, continued)

Hours: Monday–Thursday 7 a.m.–10 a.m., 4:30 p.m.–6:30 p.m., Friday 7 a.m.–10 a.m., 4:30 p.m.–7 p.m., Saturday 10:30 a.m.–1:30 p.m., 4:30 p.m.–7 p.m., Sunday 10:30 a.m.–1:30 p.m., 4:30 p.m.–6:30 p.m.

Richmond Dining Hall

Food: All-you-can-eat, cafeteria-style

Location: Ellicott Complex, North Campus

Hours: Sunday–Thursday 5 p.m.–8 p.m.

Salsa

Food: Southwest/Mexican

Location: Ellicott Complex, North Campus

Hours: Monday–Friday 11 a.m.–8 p.m.

Sizzles

Food: Breakfast and grill

Location: Ellicott Complex, North Campus

Hours: Monday–Friday 8 a.m.–5 p.m., Saturday–Sunday 11 a.m.–6 p.m.

The Tiffin Room

Food: Full-service restaurant

Location: Student Union, North Campus

Hours: Monday–Friday 11:30 a.m.–1:30 p.m.

Wrap It Up

Food: Bagels and sandwich wraps

Location: Ellicott Complex, North Campus

Hours: Monday–Friday 8 a.m.–2 p.m., Saturday–Sunday 10 a.m.–6 p.m.

Off-Campus Places to Use Your Meal Plan:

None

24-Hour On-Campus Eating?

None

Student Favorites:

Bert's

CFA Café

Harriman Café

Hubies

Did You Know?

Each quad in the Ellicott Complex **used to have its own cafeteria** because the quads were originally conceived as independent "residential colleges." Today, the cafeterias have other uses. The Spaulding cafeteria, for example, now houses the Office of Campus Parking and Transportation.

Every few weeks, **the dining halls have theme nights**, when they bring in a special chef, cook a completely unique menu, and decorate the dining hall. Italian Night, '50s Night, and Chinese New Year are some of the best ones.

Other Options

On North Campus, many students and faculty eat at the Commons, a facility adjacent to the Student Union that houses an excellent soup and sandwich shop, a Korean place, a Chinese restaurant, a full-service Italian restaurant, and Starbucks and Burger King franchises. You can't use your meal plan at these places because they're privately owned. Many South Campus denizens dine at popular eateries in University Heights (see Off-Campus Dining). Around exam time, the Munchie Machine truck gives out free food at the dorms.

Students Speak Out On...
Campus Dining

"The food in the dorms is very inconsistent. Sometimes the food is great, and sometimes the best thing to eat is cereal. The on-campus places for lunch are good."

"It's not the best you'll find, but I think **it's edible in most places**. Bert's is one of the best. Pistachio's is pretty good, Putnam's serves its purpose, and the food in the Commons is pretty decent."

"The food on campus is **awful, in every aspect**. While there are one or two places that offer decent eats, the food prices on campus are inexcusable."

"Not only do the dorms have regular dining halls, but they have a **wide variety of other food places** that sell subs, wraps, salads, tacos, fried foods, and so on. These places are open a lot later than the dining halls, too. It's a good escape because, while the dining halls are something your mom might make, these places were more like what you would find when you go to the mall."

"I really like the dining on campus. All sorts of foods are at your convenience and at a fairly reasonable price. The dining halls in Legoland (Ellicott) are **all-you-can-eat in a comfortable setting**."

"The food selection on campus increased dramatically with the opening of Ellicott Complex food court. However, the food is **expensive if you're paying cash**, and the dining hall food is stereotypical of college dining halls."

"The campus food sucks. The dining halls are always full of the **same stuff you don't want** because the quality is bad. The dining halls are very nice-looking, though, with good lighting and good seats. Ellicott dining halls are the best."

"There are a ton of things to eat, but just be careful about what you take into your body. The average college kid goes nuts during the first few weeks of school and eats only pizza and ice cream, because it's available. There are foods that won't contribute to your love handles; you just have to be smart enough to eat them. As far as taste goes, there's enough variety that **almost everyone can find something to eat**. Two tips: never eat anything called a 'Monster Burger,' and always get up in time for brunch on Saturday and Sunday mornings. Those brunches will be the best meals of your college career."

"On-campus food is bad. The cheeseburgers **give you cramps and cost $45 more than they should**. I once found a screw in my Chinese chicken."

"Other than the dining halls, you have a **wide range of food on campus** that is decent. Go to the Commons, and you'll find something good to eat."

"Overall, the food on campus is pretty good. There are tons of places all over campus to eat. **When in doubt, go to Bert's**. It's the best by far on campus, and it's only open for breakfast and lunch."

"The dining halls are decent. There is generally enough variety that **you can find something you like**. They always have pasta available, a wok, and a salad bar, which are good back-ups in case the daily menu doesn't have anything you like."

"Most of the places on the Spine, such as Putnam's, Bert's, and the CFA Café, all sell **about the same thing**. For a real change now and then, you can go to the Commons, which is not owned by the University, so the food is completely different."

"The dining hall in Governors was genuinely good my freshman year. But they got a new chef this year, and now **I can barely fill my plate** with things I want to eat."

"On-campus food is decent. The **food in the dorms is tolerable**, but it gets old quick. Bert's, by far, has the best food on campus. Putnam's, in the Student Union, has the next best food. A lot of the rest of the food for purchase in the academic buildings is very similar to the food at the Student Union."

"I would probably rate the food on campus high. There are a **great number of places to choose from**. Dining halls in the dorms have their good days and their bad days. The nice thing about the meal plans is that you can use the dining hall equivalency at some of the on-campus restaurants, which have much better food than the dining halls. I would recommend using your breakfast equivalency at Bert's in Talbert Hall. The two old men with gray mustaches make the greatest pancakes and omelets in Buffalo."

The College Prowler Take On...
Campus Dining

North Campus's isolation means students are stuck with the campus-food monopoly one to three times a day. And with a couple of exceptions, the dining options in UB's food network are bland and overpriced. The meal plans for the dining halls are expensive and less flexible than at most schools; you get a set number of meals per week, and the halls are only open for about three hours. But most students are pleased with the dining hall food (except for the Governors dining hall, where it is terrible). The staff is friendly and has a sense of humor. On Fridays during football season, they serve everything from "Rutgers Sucks Rigatoni" to "Beat Bowling Green Beans." Dozens of lunch places are scattered about the Spine because most people are at classes around noon. The bigger classroom buildings have small food courts where you can grab a quick bite between classes, and there are several large dining centers. It's satisfying for freshmen and sophomores, but older students are usually bored of the food.

The Commons, which houses the only independently-owned eateries within walking distance of the Spine, is hit or miss. The Chinese joint is lousy, but there's a good Korean place and a great deli place with a huge menu. Bert's is the student favorite for lunch. It's a crowded Talbert Hall food court with a bright and airy atrium. The scraggly old men with long curly hair and handlebar mustaches at Bert's grill have become legends on campus. Some students genuinely enjoy the campus food. But, unless they're willing to eat the same three or four things every week, most students tire of it.

B-

The College Prowler® Grade on

Campus Dining: B-

Our grade on Campus Dining addresses the quality of both school-owned dining halls and independent on-campus restaurants as well as the price, availability, and variety of food.

Off-Campus Dining

The Lowdown On... Off-Campus Dining

Restaurant Prowler: Popular Places to Eat!

Ambrosia

Food: Mediterranean

467 Elmwood Ave., West Side

(716) 881-2196

Cool Features: You can get squid or octopus as an appetizer.

Price: $20–$30 per person

Hours: Daily 7 a.m.–10 p.m., reservations recommended

Amy's Place

Food: Lebanese, American

3234 Main St., University Heights

(716) 832-6666

Cool Features: Often Amy's Place's breakfast is ranked the best in Buffalo.

Price: $10–$20 per person

Hours: Daily 6:30 a.m.–9 p.m.

➜

Anchor Bar

Food: American grill food

1047 Main St., Medical Campus

(716) 886-8920

Cool Features: Legend has it, the chicken wing was invented here in the late '60s.

Price: $5–$10 per person

Hours: Monday–Thursday 11 a.m.–11 p.m., Friday 11 a.m.–1 a.m., Saturday–Sunday 12 p.m.–1 a.m.

Coffee Bean Café

Food: Upscale American lunches, Louisiana Creole dinners, desserts

3260 Main St., University Heights

(716) 837-2326

Cool Features: New Orleans Sunday brunch with cajun-style food, piano band, and dancing; Bluegrass Mondays with bluegrass band; tall oak booths.

Price: $10–$20 per person

Hours: Sunday–Friday 8 a.m.–11 p.m., Saturday 10 a.m.–11 p.m.

Denny's

Food: American, diner

3920 Maple Rd., Amherst

(716) 446-1671

Price: $5-$10 per person

Hours: Daily 24 hours

Duff's

Food: Pizza, burgers, wings

3651 Sheridan Dr. (at Millersport Hwy.), Amherst

(716) 834-6234

Cool Features: Their wings are often voted Buffalo's best; "Suicide Wings" are rumored to be the hottest in town.

Price: $7–$15 per person

Hours: Monday–Saturday 11 a.m.–11 p.m., Sunday 12 p.m.–11 p.m.

Fat Bob's Smokehouse

Food: Southern-style barbecue

41 Virginia Pl., Allentown

(716) 887-2971

Cool Features: Fat Bob's has one of Buffalo's coolest fish tanks.

Price: $20–$25 per person

Hours: Sunday–Wednesday 11:30 a.m.–10 p.m., Thursday 11:30 a.m.–11 p.m., Friday–Saturday 11:30 a.m.–12 a.m. (Bar closes at 4 a.m. every day), reservations recommended

Gabriel's Gate

Food: American

145 Allen St., Allentown

(716) 886-0602

Price: $10–$20 per person

Hours: Monday–Wednesday 11:30 a.m.–12 a.m., Thursday 11:30 a.m.–1 a.m., Friday–Saturday 11:30 a.m.–2 a.m., Sunday 12 p.m.–12 a.m.

IHOP

Food: American, breakfast

4003 Maple Rd., Amherst

(716) 446-1117

Price: $5-$10 per person

Hours: Daily 24 hours

India Gate

Food: Indian

1116 Elmwood Ave., West Side

(716) 886-4000

Cool Features: Lunch buffet.

Price: $10–$25 per person

Hours: Daily 11:30 a.m.–2:30 p.m., 4:30 p.m.–10 p.m.

Jasmine Thai

Food: Thai

1330 Niagara Falls Blvd.

(716) 838-3011

Price: $10–$25 per person

Hours: Monday–Friday 11:30 a.m.–9:30 p.m., Saturday–Sunday 12 p.m.–9:30 p.m.

Jim's SteakOut

Food: Steak hoagies and chicken fingers

3094 Main St., University Heights

(716) 838-6666

Cool Features: Jim's serves Buffalo's greasiest subs, including the Diavlo, a roast beef and hot pepper sub.

Price: $5–$10 per person

Hours: Daily 10 a.m.–5 a.m.

Just Pizza

Food: Pizza

3172 Main St., University Heights

(716) 831-9979

Cool Features: Just Pizza, which serves trademark Buffalo pizza, has almost a dozen different kinds of crusts, including the popular sesame crust.

Price: $5–$10 per person

Hours: Sunday–Wednesday 10 a.m.–12 a.m., Thursday 10 a.m.–2 a.m., Friday 10 a.m.–3 a.m., Saturday 10 a.m.–5 a.m.

Lake Effect Diner

Food: American diner food

3165 Main St., University Heights

(716) 833-1952

Cool Features: Lake Effect, a classic American diner, is open all day and all night. They also have a take-out menu and daily specials.

Price: $7–$15 per person

Hours: Daily 24 hours

Left Bank

Food: French, Continental

511 Rhode Island Ave., West Side

(716) 882-3509

Price: $30–$40 per person

Hours: Sunday–Saturday 5 p.m.–10 p.m., Sunday brunch 11 a.m.–3 p.m. (reservations strongly recommended)

Mighty Taco

Food: Mexican fast food

2309 Eggert Rd. (at Sheridan Dr.), Tonawanda

(716) 833-3060

Cool Features: Most people swear that Mighty Taco is ten times better than Taco Bell.

Price: $5–$10 per person

Hours: Sunday–Thursday 10 a.m.–1 a.m., Friday–Saturday 10 a.m.–2 a.m.

Ming Teh

Food: Chinese

126 Niagra Blvd., Fort Erie, Ontario

(905) 871-7971

Price: $12–$30 per person

Hours: Daily 11 a.m.–11 p.m.

Nektar

Food: Mediterranean, martini bar

451 Elmwood Ave., West Side

(716) 881-1829

Cool Features: While they're expensive, Nektar has Buffalo's best specialty drinks.

Price: $30–$40 per person

Hours: Monday–Saturday 11 a.m.–2:30 a.m., closed Sunday, reservations strongly recommended

O Restaurant and Lounge

Food: Japanese

Northtown Plaza, Sheridan Dr., Amherst

(716) 332-4656

Price: $20–$30 per person

Hours: Monday–Friday 11:30 a.m.–2 a.m., Saturday 4:30 p.m.–2 a.m.

Outback Steakhouse

Food: Steak, grill, seafood

1551 Niagra Falls Blvd.

(716) 833-6067

Price: $12–$20 per person

Hours: Monday–Thursday 4 p.m.–10:30 p.m., Friday 4 p.m.–11:30 p.m., Saturday 3 p.m.–11:30 p.m., Sunday 3 p.m.–10 p.m.

Pano's

Food: Greek, American

1081 Elmwood Ave., West Side

(716) 886-9081

Price: $7–$15 per person

Hours: Daily 24 hours

Sal's Pizzeria

Food: Pizza

3171 Main St., Amherst

(716) 838-0800

Price: $8–$12 per person

Hours: Sunday–Thursday 11 a.m.–4 p.m., Friday–Saturday 11 a.m.–5 p.m.

Ted's Hot Dogs

Food: Grill

2312 Sheridan Dr., Tonawanda

(716) 834-6287

Price: Under $10 per person

Hours: Monday–Sunday 10:30 a.m.–11 p.m.

Tom's Restaurant

Food: Greek, American diner food

3221 Sheridan Dr., Amherst

(716) 837-7310

Cool Features: Tom's serves great Greek food and is open 24 hours.

Price: $7–$15 per person

Hours: Daily 24 hours

Towne

Food: Greek

186 Allen St. (at Elmwood Ave.), Allentown

(716) 884-5128

(Towne, continued)

Cool Features: Towne has a popular deck in the summer that has a nice view of the crowds on Allen Street.

Price: $10–$20 per person

Hours: Daily 24 hours

Tsunami

Food: Asian fusion

1141 Kenmore Ave., Kenmore

(716) 447-7915

Price: $25–$35 per person

Hours: Monday–Thursday 5 p.m.–10 p.m., Saturday–Sunday 5 p.m.–11 p.m.

Zetti's Pizza & Pasta

Food: Italian

3500 Main St., Amherst

(716) 447-7915

http://zettis.com

Price: $10–$16 per person

Hours: Daily 10:30 a.m.–11 p.m.

Did You Know?

According to legend, **chicken wings were invented** at Buffalo's fabled Anchor Bar, five miles from campus. Buffalo wings are bigger, hotter, crispier on the outside, and juicier on the inside than at any place in the world.

In Buffalo, waitresses won't blink if you ask for **vinegar with your fries**—it's a Canadian tradition.

Student Favorites:

Amy's Place

Duff's

Mighty Taco

Jim's SteakOut

Just Pizza

Pano's

24-Hour Eating:

Denny's

IHOP

Lake Effect Diner

Pano's

Tom's Restaurant

Towne

Closest Grocery Stores:

North Campus:

Wegmans Alberta Drive

675 Alberta Dr. (at Maple Road), Amherst

(716) 831-6300

Tops International

3980 Maple Rd., Amherst

(716) 515-0075

South Campus:

Tops University Plaza

3500 Main St., University Heights

(716) 515-3240

Best Pizza:

Just Pizza (Chicago-style)

Zetti's Pizza & Pasta (New York-style)

Best Chinese:

Ming Teh (Fort Erie)

Best Breakfast:

Amy's Place

Best Wings:

Anchor Bar, Duff's

Best Healthy:

Jasmine Thai

Best Place to Take Your Parents:

Nektar

Other Places to Check Out:

Anderson's

Applebee's

Bennigan's

Chang's Garden

Chili's

Fuddruckers

Joe Mata's

My Tomato Pie

The Spot

TGI Friday's

Ya Ya's

Students Speak Out On...
Off-Campus Dining

"From right off campus to downtown, there are classy Italian restaurants, Asian restaurants, and hamburger places. Two of my favorites are Amy's Place on Main Street and Gabriel's Gate on Allen Street."

"If there's only one thing Buffalo is known for, it's our food. The first stop on anyone's list should be the Anchor Bar, **home of the original chicken wing**. Some chicken-wing connoisseurs will tell you that Duff's has the best wings in town. Those people are bold-faced liars. Go for the original—Anchor Bar all the way. Aside from chicken wings, Buffalo cuisine is incredible. The independent restaurants in the area are full of charm and atmosphere. The Allentown district is home to my personal favorites; any restaurant you try along that strip is sure to please."

"The Spot on Elmwood Avenue is the best coffee shop I have ever been to. Though it's expensive, **you can order anything you desire** and sit on a cushy couch while you jive about your java."

"Buffalo **restaurants are almost all chains**—Applebee's, Chili's, TGI Friday's, and Bennigan's. You won't find good mom-and-pop food here. I like pizza, bagels, and delis, which they have none of up here."

"The restaurants around Buffalo are pretty good, generally. You can find **almost any type of food** you're looking for if you're willing to scour the phone book. Some of the best restaurants around are Duff's (wings), Ya-Ya's (Cajun), and My Tomato Pie (Italian)."

"**Buffalo's fat**, and I don't think you'll find any native who's going to complain about it. There's some really great food here. For the ultimate best Beef on Weck (and don't be one of those dorks who asks, 'What the heck is weck?'—learn it, live it, love it), you have to head over to Charlie the butcher's on Cayuga Road and Wehrle Drive. It's the best in homemade comfort food and stick-to-your-ribs ooey-gooeyness."

"Off-campus food is great **if you know where to go**. Mighty Taco is probably the cheapest food in the city, but it is delicious and very addicting. Ted's Hot Dogs has the best hot dogs I've had in my life. Anderson's is the place to go for ice cream—cones are half off when it's snowing out. There are also some good Chinese places. One on Maple Road is called Chang's Garden. It's a sit-down place and a bit more formal than the average Chinese place, but the service is fast, good, and pleasing as long as you can understand the waiter."

"Head over to Peace Bridge and take a right into Fort Erie. The best Chinese food in the area is at a little tiny place known as Ming Teh. It's got the **most delicious Chinese cuisine** as well as the best on-the-water viewpoint of the Buffalo skyline."

"There are many **chain restaurants just a mile or two** off North Campus. There are also many great places to eat in the city. If you're looking to take a girl out on a first date, try Ambrosia."

"Food is the best part of Buffalo. The best food is probably by the bars. Sal's Pizza has a New York City flavor, while Jim's SteakOut is a combination of Subway and McDonalds on steroids. So many places are **open all hours of the night** for late-night munchies, with decent prices, since it's fairly inexpensive to open anything in Buffalo."

"Buffalo has great food selection at all times of the day and **for all price ranges**. Duff's, right near the campus, has the greatest chicken wings ever (why do you think they call them Buffalo wings?). Mighty Taco is one of my favorites for a cheap, quick meal. From Gabriel's Gate and Fat Bob's Smokehouse in Allentown, to Pano's (open late) on Elmwood near Buff State, to Joe Mata's on Transit Road, the choices of places to eat is endless. Along Niagara Falls Boulevard, about two miles from campus, there are dozens of chain restaurants, if that's your thing, but personally, I prefer the locally-owned places."

"Buffalo **restaurants are very, very good**. If the Buffalo population knows anything, it's good eating."

The College Prowler Take On...
Off-Campus Dining

Some kids from New York City complain that you can't find a good bagel or deli in Buffalo. That's the only gripe you'll hear from anyone who has experienced the local food. Buffalo is not one of the 10 most overweight cities in America by accident. Fine dining and cheap eats are both top-notch. There are dozens of classy restaurants, including adventurous new openings every year; though, except for the annual parents' visit, cheap eating is the rule for most local students. Rumor has it that there are more pizzerias per capita in Buffalo than anywhere else. In keeping with the city's Midwestern ethos, Buffalo pizza is made Chicago-style, with a thick, doughy crust. Sal's and Zetti's in the Heights cater to the New York-style pizza crowd, but thin-crust pies are hard to find in most parts of the city. Though chicken wings were invented at the Anchor Bar near downtown, many students say they have been perfected at Duff's in Amherst. You know a place is serious when they tell you how hot the wings are by printing the Scoville units of each sauce in the menu.

Beef on weck sandwiches, made with roast beef and gravy on a salted kümmelweck roll, are as common as cheeseburgers in Buffalo. And students rave about Mighty Taco, a local Mexican chain that serves dirt-cheap tacos and burritos. Several places in the Heights offer a $0.99 or $1.99 breakfast, including Amy's Place, where the Lebanese breakfasts often earn honors for best breakfast in town. Coffee shops are not as plentiful as they are in bigger cities. But Buffalo has some good ones, such as Coffee Bean in the Heights, which serves savory Creole food and a popular New Orleans Sunday brunch. Amherst's wide suburban boulevards are peppered with your average chains like Fuddruckers and Outback Steakhouse and high-quality Indian, Thai, Vietnamese, and Japanese restaurants. For some reason, though, there are relatively few good Chinese places. Buffalo could also use a few more 24-hour dining options and a couple of genuinely good delicatessens close to campus.

A-

The College Prowler® Grade on

Off-Campus Dining: A-

A high Off-Campus Dining grade implies that off-campus restaurants are affordable, accessible, and worth visiting. Other factors include the variety of cuisine and the availability of alternative options (vegetarian, vegan, Kosher, etc.).

Campus Housing

The Lowdown On... Campus Housing

Best Dorms:
Ellicott Complex
Goodyear Hall

Worst Dorms:
Macdonald
Pritchard
Schoellkopf Halls

Undergrads Living on Campus:
38%

Number of Dormitories:
8

Number of University-Owned Apartments:
3 available to undergraduates

→

Dormitories:

Clement Hall

Location: South Campus

Floors: 10

Total Occupancy: 480

Bathrooms: Private

Coed: Yes

Residents: Freshmen, sophomores, juniors, seniors

Room Types: Suites (two doubles connected by a bathroom)

Special Features: Laundry, study lounge, TV lounge, computer lab, aerobics and fitness room

Ellicott Complex (Fargo, Porter, Richmond, Red Jacket, Spaulding, and Wilkeson Quads)

Location: North Campus

Floors: Each quad contains eight to ten buildings that range from five to ten stories

Total Occupancy: 3,250

Bathrooms: Communal

Coed: Yes

Residents: Freshmen, sophomores, juniors, seniors

Room Types: Singles, doubles, triples, split triples, quads, split quads

Special Features: Laundry, food court, aerobics and fitness room, computer lab, study center, convenience store

Flint Village Apartments

Location: North Campus

Floors: 3

Total Occupancy: 536

Bathrooms: Private

Coed: Yes

Residents: Sophomores, juniors, seniors

Room Types: One-, two-, and four-bedroom apartments

Special Features: Laundry, community center with reception room, lounge, game room

Goodyear Hall

Location: South Campus

Floors: 10

Total Occupancy: 480

Bathrooms: Private

Coed: Yes

Residents: Freshmen

Room Types: Suites (two doubles connected by a bathroom)

Special Features: Laundry, study lounge, TV lounge, computer lab, aerobics and fitness room

Governors Residence Halls (Dewey, Lehman, Clinton, and Roosevelt Halls)

Location: North Campus

Floors: 3

Total Occupancy: 825

Bathrooms: Communal

Coed: Yes

(Governors Residence Halls, continued)

Residents: Freshmen, sophomores, juniors, seniors

Room Types: Singles, doubles

Special Features: Laundry, aerobics and fitness room, computer lab, study center, convenience store

Hadley Village Apartments

Location: North Campus

Floors: 3

Total Occupancy: 624

Bathrooms: Private

Coed: Yes

Residents: Sophomores, juniors, seniors

Room Types: Four-bedroom apartments

Special Features: Laundry, community center with reception room, lounge, game room

MacDonald Hall

Location: South Campus

Floors: 4

Total Occupancy: 140

Bathrooms: Communal

Coed: Yes

Residents: Freshmen, sophomores, juniors, seniors

Room Types: Singles, doubles

Special Features: Laundry, study lounge

Michael Hall

Location: South Campus

Floors: 4

Total Occupancy: 140

Bathrooms: Communal

Coed: Yes

Residents: Freshmen, sophomores, juniors, seniors

Room Types: Singles, doubles

Special Features: Laundry, study lounge

Pritchard Hall

Location: South Campus

Floors: 4

Total Occupancy: 140

Bathrooms: Communal

Coed: Yes

Residents: Freshmen, sophomores, juniors, seniors

Room Types: Singles, doubles

Special Features: Laundry, study lounge

Schoellkopf Hall

Location: South Campus

Floors: 4

Total Occupancy: 140

Bathrooms: Communal

Coed: Yes

Residents: Freshmen, sophomores, juniors, seniors

Room Types: Singles, doubles

Special Features: Laundry, study lounge

South Lake Village Apartments

Location: North Campus

Floors: 2-3

Total Occupancy: 552

Bathrooms: Private

Coed: Yes

Residents: Sophomores, juniors, seniors

Room Types: Studio, one-, two- and four-bedroom apartments

Special Features: Laundry, community center with reception room, lounge, game room

Housing Offered:

Singles: 9%
Doubles: 35%
Triples/Suites: 18%
Apartments: 29%
Other: 9%

Room Types

Singles: Student has his or her own room. Offered at high prices and limited quantity in Pritchard Hall, MacDonald Hall, and Ellicott Complex dorms.

Doubles: Two students share a room. Offered in Clement and Goodyear Halls where each double shares a bathroom, and in the Ellicott Complex dorms.

Suites: Some Ellicott Complex rooms, particularly in the towers, share a common room; however, these "split quads" (two doubles) or "split triples" (a double and a single) go quickly to sophomores, juniors, and seniors with low lottery numbers.

Triples and Quads: In the Ellicott Complex, some freshmen and sophomores live three or four to a room. Some quads come with their own bathrooms.

Five apartment complex "villages" are located on or near North Campus. Three are available to undergraduates. The application process is highly competitive; it's impossible for a freshman to get in and nearly impossible for a sophomore. Units range from studios to four-bedroom suites.

Bed Type

33 in. x 80 in.

Available for Rent

Mini refrigerators

Also Available

Special-interest housing

Cleaning Service?

All public areas in residence halls and apartments are cleaned. Bathrooms are cleaned in the dorms but not the apartments.

What You Get

In the dorms, you get a desk, chair, mirror, mattress, and bed you can loft. Apartments are fully furnished. They come with a closet, double bed, nightstand, dresser, cable jack, and data port in the bedrooms, refrigerator, dishwasher, garbage disposal, stove, microwave, storage cabinets and recycling/trash bins in the kitchens, a couch, chairs and a cable jack in the living rooms, an intercom system, and air conditioning.

Did You Know?

All campus residents **get free cable and access to three movie channels**, which play everything from new releases to classics.

Governors Residence Halls **are designed by noted architect IM Pei**, who also designed Boston's John Hancock Tower and the East Wing of the National Gallery in Washington. However, few students think his dull concrete dorm at UB compares to the quality of his other work.

Laundry **is free on campus**. Because many students who live off campus have to pay for their laundry, non-residents sometimes bring their laundry to North or South Campus and try to use the laundry rooms in the dorms.

Students Speak Out On...
Campus Housing

"The dorms are all right. I live in Governors, and I really love it here. I highly recommend staying a night in the dorms if you're deciding whether or not to come here—it's the only way you really get a feel for the place."

"Like the academic programs, the dorms are **what you make of them**. Although most of the rooms are cramped and dimly lit, a used couch or a futon with a tapestry or two can turn what originally looks like a higher-grade prison cell into a respectable living quarter."

"The first thing you and your roommates should buy is a **futon, which is key** because it is your couch as well as the shack-up bed."

"Dorms—not so hot. Go to a private school if you want nice ones. Tiny rooms, ugly little floors, cinder block walls; but **the décor doesn't really matter because you'll treasure the experience anyway**."

"The dorms are excellent. Legoland (also known as Ellicott) has over 3,000 students housed under its roofs, and it provides a safe atmosphere for both the sane and the wild. It has an urban feeling because there are **so many people to meet** and there is so much to do."

"The Governors Complex was designed by IM Pei, who also designed the addition to the Louvre in Paris. With such high standards, you'd think the complex would be a dream. It's not, unless your dreams include being locked in a maze that never ends. **There's nothing distinguished about Governors**, which is a series of interconnecting identical suites. After an entire year, I still got lost finding my way to the dining hall. On the upside, though, it's quiet and clean."

"The dorms have their problems, such as the annoying drunk who gets a full ride for football and doesn't go to any of his classes. But they also have their benefits, such as nice living, a **decent amount of good people**, and coed floors. I would recommend getting a quad or triple room because they are more spacious and you can live with one person you already know and still meet someone new."

"I always thought the dorms were decent. They gave you nice wooden furniture that gave the room a homier feel to it. The rooms in Ellicott were decently sized, and each room was shaped somewhat differently to **give it a unique appeal**. Governors is the dorm I would avoid the most."

"Ellicott, which everyone says **looks like a stack of Legos**, is kind of like Governors's messier little brother. He was the one who never cleaned his room and didn't really care if he showered that day. It's loud, it's fun, and my GPA is glad I didn't live there. I don't think I would have ever gotten anything done."

"The dorms are nice. I like them better than the dorms at University at Albany, where I transferred from. They are bigger, newer, and more human. This is the **main reason why I came to UB**—I loved the dorms."

"The dorms are okay. I wouldn't describe them as anything more than that. I think the experience in the dorms depends **more on the people you live with** than the type of room you live in. Triples and quads are large, but either way, there isn't a ton of space between you and your roommates, so you better like them. The on-campus apartments are very expensive. I'd live off campus before living there. All utilities are included in the monthly rent, but that still doesn't justify their high price."

"**The dorms are actually not too bad**. I really enjoyed my experience. There are two different dorms: Governors, which is known for its smart honors students, and Ellicott, which is for everyone else. The trick in Ellicott is to room away from the first three floors—they all connect, and that is where the dorms are the loudest."

"The dorms aren't bad, and they're getting better every year. Although there is a huge student population at UB, there is a great sense of community on each floor in the dorms, and **friends are easily made**. Living off campus provides a lot more freedom, space, fun, and saves a ton of money, though. For anyone able, I recommend moving into a house when you get the chance."

"Dorms are offered on both campuses, so you can choose to live in the suburbs or in the city. The on-campus apartments are very nice, but also very expensive. Ellicott is one of the **largest dorms at any college**, which is nice because friends are often close by. But with so many people, late-night fire drills are all the more common."

"Get in **Governors if you like to study**, or if you just like your peace and quiet. I've lived there for two years, and I love it because I don't have much tolerance for late-night tomfoolery in the middle of the week. If you're up for that and you're looking for a more exciting place, go to Ellicott. Stay off South Campus if you can avoid it."

The College Prowler Take On...
Campus Housing

Only about one-third of undergraduates live on campus, so rooming at "Smellicott," "Gover-nerds," or South Campus is an experience within an experience at UB. Anarchy reigns at Wilkeson Quad and Spaulding Quad in Ellicott, where many first-year students are assigned. The sheer size of Ellicott is intimidating. The complex has six quads, and each quad is its own set of eight to ten interconnected buildings that range from five to ten stories. Athletes and honors students are sent to Governors, a quieter and more intimate complex close to the academic buildings. The aging South Campus dorms are also home to a fair number of first-year undergrads who study on North. Overall, dorm living at UB is not without its quality of life issues, as rooms are crowded and false fire alarms are a constant annoyance. Everyone praises the free laundry, the availability of special-interest floors, and the campus bus service that shuttles students to and from the academic buildings. Most students love their experience in the dorms without having any special affection for the dorms themselves.

Staying in Ellicott or Governors for four years is somewhat of a stigma at UB. After sophomore year, many students take their chances in the highly competitive lottery for UB's coveted on-campus apartments. Students have to pay their dues to get an apartment. Each applicant is given a lottery number based on GPA, credit hours taken, and number of semesters in the dorms. It's clear why the apartments are in such high demand. They are handsome, modern, and convenient. Perhaps the most popular apartment complex is South Lake Village, which has stunning views every night of the sun setting behind the campus across Lake LaSalle. Two of UB's best apartment complexes, however, are available only to graduate students.

B-

The College Prowler® Grade on

Campus Housing: B-

A high Campus Housing grade indicates that dorms are clean, well-maintained, and spacious. Other determining factors include variety of dorms, proximity to classes, and social atmosphere.

Off-Campus Housing

The Lowdown On...
Off-Campus Housing

Undergrads Living in Off-Campus Housing:
62%

Best Time to Look for a Place:
Late February and March of spring semester, though units are available through the summer.

→

Average Rent For:

Studio Apartment:

Amherst/
Tonawanda: $500/mo.

North Buffalo/
West Side: $400/mo.

University Heights: $200/mo.

One-Bedroom Apartment:

Amherst/
Tonawanda: $550/mo.

North Buffalo/
West Side: $450/mo.

University Heights: $220/mo.

Two-Bedroom Apartment:

Amherst/
Tonawanda: $700/mo.

North Buffalo/
West Side: $600/mo.

University Heights: $400/mo.

Popular Areas:

Allentown (Buffalo)

Amherst

North Buffalo

Parkside (Buffalo)

Tonawanda

University Heights (Buffalo)

West Side (Buffalo)

For Assistance Contact

Sub-Board I Office of Off-Campus Housing

www.subboard.com/och

(716) 829-2224

rosario2@buffalo.edu

dgpatel@buffalo.edu

Students Speak Out On...
Off-Campus Housing

"Off-campus housing is very convenient, considering all the good bars are on South Campus and some popular classes, like Nutrition, are offered on South."

"Living off campus after freshman year is one of the smartest things I've done in my four years at UB. Living in University Heights, you are closer to the social scene of bars and frat parties. Plus, you **never have to worry about an RA** knocking on your door or finding a ride back to the dorms."

"For those who like a quiet area, there are many off-campus locations away from the Heights where students live. The Colony Apartments, right off North Campus, are a really **safe and quiet apartment complex** where many people are happy living."

"Most people who move off campus get a house in University Heights. It is a lot of fun; however, **I recommend you research your landlord** to make sure they are good. A deadbeat landlord can be a major pain. But living off campus is still a great time."

"I moved to Amherst after my freshman year—sick of RAs and quiet hours. Apartments in Amherst are everywhere, though **they're a little pricey**. Once you travel further from campus, the apartments become cheaper and, I think, much better."

"University Heights is the **greatest place to live** imaginable. The floors are crooked, the roofs are leaky, and the rent can be paid in pistachio shells. There's always a party down the block or a neighbor to lend a hand when your car gets stuck in the snow. There's no better sense of community than in the Heights."

"Most people live in the Heights, which is about five miles away from North Campus. The best housing is probably the duplexes you can rent. **They are like real condos**, and they're hooked up nice. You'll need a car, however."

"If you're the kind of person that can just **laugh it off when you blow a fuse for the tenth time in one day**, and you get entertainment at the end of the night out of watching drunk students fall down, then the Heights is the place for you. It really can be a fun place to live because the area always seems to be buzzing with activity."

"Buses that run from South Campus **make the commute easier** if you don't want to drive in the snow. Sometimes, when you are the only person on the bus, it feels like you're a rock star on tour and you have your own personal limo service."

The College Prowler Take On...
Off-Campus Housing

Off-campus housing at UB is the rule, not the exception. There are so many options off campus that where you choose to live after freshman year becomes a statement about who you are. It's common for freshmen to hear things like, "You're a real Elmwood girl," or "I can totally see you living in the Heights someday." The most popular options are the big brick houses and wooden shacks in University Heights, the cookie-cutter suburban apartments that surround North Campus, and nicer apartments on the tree-lined streets of city neighborhoods such as North Buffalo, Allentown, and the Elmwood Village.

University Heights, which spreads out for a full square mile around South Campus, has been a lively, diverse student neighborhood since the early 20th century. Though most of the academic departments moved to North Campus in the '70s, the frat houses, bars, stores, and coffee shops in the Heights are still the epicenter of off-campus social life. Thousands of students are attracted to the area for its dirt-cheap rents (usually around $200/month) and party-ready student houses. The Heights isn't for everyone, though; the threat of crime means that students ought to be street smart, and the high number of shoddy houses and slumlords means you need to really shop around. Students who think the Heights is a squalid ghetto move into Amherst apartments. Amherst places are safer, cleaner, and more convenient to campus; but they are far more expensive on average and pretty removed from the "college experience." Many urban types—art majors, theater majors, and English majors—move to one of Buffalo's upscale West Side neighborhoods. Rents are a bit steeper here, but the neighborhoods are safe (and more importantly for these students, they're trendy).

A-

The College Prowler® Grade on

Off-Campus Housing: A-

A high grade in Off-Campus Housing indicates that apartments are of high quality, close to campus, affordable, and easy to secure.

Diversity

The Lowdown On... Diversity

Native Americans:
Less than 1%

Asian American:
9%

African American:
7%

Hispanic:
4%

White:
73%

Unknown:
1%

International:
6%

Out-of-State:
2%

Political Activity

UB's protest culture has cooled since the late 1960s, when South Campus was the scene of some of the nation's most violent Vietnam War protests. Legend has it that North Campus was designed with few central gathering spaces to limit protest activity. Today, UB's political scene is relatively quiet, and protests, while often creative, are sparsely attended. The majority of students and professors are liberal Democrats, and it's not easy to be an outspoken conservative at UB. When the College Republicans held an anti-affirmative action bake sale last year, the Black Student Union, Hip Hop SA, and student government officials came out to protest.

Gay Pride

UB has an open and vibrant queer culture. Outspoken gay students can join any number of organizations, including the University's chapter of LGBTA. More quiet gay students find the privacy offered by UB's large campus to be liberating.

Most Popular Religions

UB has several large Christian groups. Because many Buffalo natives trace their ancestry to Ireland, Italy, and Eastern Europe, the campus's Catholic organizations (including the Newman Center) are particularly active. There are also several Hindu and Muslim student organizations.

Economic Status

Most UB students are solidly middle class; they drive used cars and pay for their own tuition and housing. Hardly anybody cares about where your parents work, what you wear, or how much money you have. There are a few very rich people and few very poor people. Students from the New York City area tend to be wealthier.

Minority Clubs

UB has nearly 50 minority clubs. The most active groups include the Black Student Union, the Chinese Student Association, the Indian Student Association, and the Latin American Student Association. Each group organizes several major cultural events each year.

Students Speak Out On...
Diversity

"UB is the most diverse place I have ever seen. UB has a significant Asian and Indian population, as well as a slew of other ethnic groups. It's pretty cool when you think that you probably won't live with a diverse group of people like this again in your life."

"UB is very diverse. Though the actual percentages of the ethnic breakdown might not be impressive, there is certainly **no lack of ethnic and racial diversity** on campus. However, if integration is what you're looking for, you might not find that here—you might not find that anywhere. People pretty much stick to their own, except for those occasions when events like the International Fiesta bring us together to cheer each other as we celebrate our cultures."

"The campus is very diverse, but a lot of **people hang out in their own groups**: the Asians with the Asians, the whites with the whites, blacks with blacks, and so on. It's really a shame."

"UB was recently named the tenth most diverse campus in the nation. It's ironic, since Buffalo was also named the eighth most segregated city. I've been **opened up to a world of cultural education** at UB, and I have made friends of all ages, races, and cultures. It's kind of lame, but I couldn't have asked for a better school to learn about differences and similarities at the same time."

"The campus is surprisingly very diverse. That's what makes UB such a great place to spend time. It's so interesting; **it's worth hanging around after your day is over**, just to meet the many different people from all over the world."

"UB has students from every race, and there are many international students, as well. People will usually make friends with people from **many different races and countries**, but the closest social groups usually are not mixed. It is common to walk through the Student Union and see races separated by tables."

"There's a good mix of guys and girls from all cultures. You can meet all new types of **people from all over the world**—including Canadians—giving you new insights every day."

"The campus is extremely diverse. It was a bit of a shock for me, honestly. I graduated with a class of 80 kids, and there was one black kid. While I can appreciate other cultures, **it can take some time to get used to hearing other dialects of English all the time**."

"I can't imagine the campus being more diverse. You can walk through the Spine and hear **at least eight different languages** being spoken as you walk."

"UB is indeed a very diverse campus, but at times, it may seem cliquey. You are sometimes **just a face in the crowd** here, but if you thrive on meeting new people and just getting out there, then this is the place for you."

The College Prowler Take On...
Diversity

Students from all over the world come to Buffalo, particularly for the prestigious engineering and computer science programs. It's the norm for students to hear several different languages and to see several different styles of dress as they walk from class to class. Ethnic student groups are major institutions that spend their sizable budgets on showy festivals and cultural celebrations. Just because nearly all the American students are from New York State doesn't mean they are not a diverse group—Latinos from New York City, upper-middle-class kids from the parts of Long Island where *The Great Gatsby* was set strong, silent types from the Adirondack foothills, Jamaican Americans from Jamaica, Queens, and middle-class suburban kids from all over the state. Some kids drive BMWs that they got as birthday presents, while others take the campus buses and work part-time jobs just to pay their tuition. UB's lesbian, gay, bisexual, and transgender community is visible and influential, and there are dozens of student religious groups.

While everyone treasures the diversity, most people at UB don't have any illusions about the poor state of ethnic integration on campus. Real flare-ups (shouting matches and bar fights) are more likely to ensue between upstate and downstate factions than people from different races. Most student groups are informally segregated, and while American students often learn a lot about other cultures, such learning is often passive, like learning about the weather by looking out the window. Some international students study in the U.S. out of necessity and give Americans a cold shoulder. And some Americans, at their worst, apply negative stereotypes to foreign students. UB's diversity is impressive and exciting but somewhat superficial.

B-

The College Prowler® Grade on

Diversity: B-

A high grade in Diversity indicates that ethnic minorities and international students have a notable presence on campus and that students of different economic backgrounds, religious beliefs, and sexual preferences are well-represented.

Guys & Girls

The Lowdown On... Guys & Girls

Men Undergrads:
54%

Women Undergrads:
46%

Birth Control Available?

Birth control for men and women is available—everything from condoms to the morning-after pill.

Most Prevalent STDs on Campus

Chlamydia, gonorrhea, syphilis, herpes

Social Scene

Enrolling at UB from high school is like moving from a small town to a big city, or going from the bar in *Cheers* to a sprawling dance club. It's easy to meet people, but it's also easy to feel alienated. Students who live on campus join clubs or play sports, and they have no problem making friends and meeting guys and girls. But it's still easy for quiet students to get lost. While most students are genuinely friendly, few people will want to get to know you just because you're in the same school. If you commute from home and don't join any activities, you'll have a hard time meeting people.

Hookups or Relationships?

To some new students, the lively bar scene in Buffalo and Niagara Falls means one thing: hooking up. Random hookups are relatively common. However, because students tend to make a few close friends rather than form large cliques, it's not uncommon for older students to be in long-term relationships. Some older, single students complain that all good-looking upperclassmen are dating a long-term boyfriend or girlfriend. That's why it's so common for upperclassmen guys to hook up with freshman girls.

Best Place to Meet Guys/Girls

Students who live on campus have the luxury of meeting girls and guys in all the classic college settings: gyms, dorms, dining halls, and (if you're lucky and smooth) laundry rooms and computer labs. Commuters often have trouble meeting guys and girls unless they join activities, play sports, or go out on the weekends. And it's tough to meet people in class, period. Nine times out of ten, asking out the guy or girl from whom you borrow notes when you skip class is a recipe for disaster.

Aside from clubs and activities, the best place to meet people is the University Heights bar and party scene. It's not only where most students go to hook up, it's where to get to know people from class or the dorms in a more casual atmosphere. Though UB is a large school, it's surprising how many familiar faces you'll see on a weekend night in the Heights. If you play your cards right, you'll get at least a phone number or two.

Did You Know?

Top Places to Find Hotties:

1. Heights bars and Chippewa clubs
2. Off-campus parties
3. Big student organizations (e.g. Schussmeisters, the ski club)

Top Places to Hook Up:

1. Off-campus parties
2. University Heights bars between 2 a.m. and 4 a.m.
3. Cheap hotels in Niagara Falls, Canada
4. The dorms (including lounges)
5. The campus's hidden places, such as Kanazawa Island and Baird Point

Dress Code

While you'll find interesting fashions on the fringes, most UB students take a bohemian approach to clothing. A majority of students wear jeans to class with hoodies, long-sleeve T-shirts, or untucked button-downs. Steve & Barry's, a national chain of stores that sells college sweats for under $10, became an immediate sensation when they opened a Buffalo location. A general rule is that for every student wearing Ralph Lauren or Kenneth Cole, there's someone who gets their threads off discount racks at local thrift stores. However, a few downstate students, sport absolutely cutting-edge fashions. And if you're in a large lecture class, you're likely to have at least a dozen people with Mohawks, fishnets, unusual tattoos, or odd piercings.

Students Speak Out On...
Guys & Girls

"Be sure to check out all the hot chicks in the first few weeks of school while it's still warm, before they all migrate south for the winter. But be sure to avoid Long Island girls. They tend to be a bit pretentious."

"There is an incredible array of females at UB. There are nerdy girls who have clearly never had an orgasm; then, there are girls who want nothing more than to ride your rocket, as long as you've got some musky cologne and some Hollister in your closet. There are some cute emo girls, plastic glasses and one-inch buttons included. You have to figure **there's someone worthwhile** at a school with 30,000 students."

"The guys are **mostly crappy Abercrombie dudes**. The girls are mostly headband-wearing, sweatpants-rocking, accent-bearing idiots."

"There is no lack of **lovely faces at this institution**. Lovely black faces, lovely Latin faces, lovely white faces, lovely Asian faces. Every now and again, the flow of lovely faces will be interrupted by a not-so-lovely face, and then it's back to lovely faces. Lovely nerd faces, lovely athlete faces, lovely emo-faces. And just when you thought you couldn't get enough of the loveliness, spring comes and the coats come off."

"The girls in Buffalo **are like the wings**: the mild ones are hot, the medium ones are very hot, and the hot ones are very, very hot."

"The social scene at UB is interesting. **Avoiding the Long Island girls is a must**. They are nothing but a pain, and you feel dumber just having heard or witnessed a conversation between two of them. Hotness is hard to tell most of the time because most people are layered up pretty good to fight the winds that always terrorize North Campus."

"UB has **three sub-species of girls**: 1) The College Girl. She wears jeans and a sweater to school and doesn't care what anyone thinks of her. She is 5'6". 2) The Art Girl. She wears a lot of makeup and dresses in black. She wears a lot of stripes and usually dyes her hair black with a fringy mod cut. She wears thick-rimmed brown fashion glasses. She doesn't date or talk to people. They don't understand her art. 3) The Long Island Girl. It is required by her sorority that she has at least six inches of stomach showing at all times, in winter or in summer. She is never without her pointed toe shoes, headband, or sweatpants. She also carries a small purse, slung over her right arm. She hangs out at the Steer on Fridays and Quote on Saturdays."

"The frat guys and sorority girls are full of themselves. Overall, there is a **50 percent attractiveness rate**."

"There are a lot of girls who have nothing in their heads, and there's a minority of girls who are worth your time. While there are smart, good-looking girls at UB, **you'll have to dig pretty deep** to find them."

"I think only hot girls go to this college. Go to Canada. Over there, the girls try to pick you up. It's amazing. **Everyone usually gets some** here at UB, so if that's your thing, Buffalo is the perfect fit for you."

"There are two kinds of guys at UB: **guys who look like trolls and guys who do not look like trolls**. Somehow, both the trolls and the non-trolls end up with fairly good-looking girls. The guy doesn't even have to have two eyes or hair, and he can get a decent-looking chick. It boggles my mind, as does the large contingent of guys at UB who tan."

"After a long, cold winter, springtime in Buffalo is great because all the **hot chicks come out from hiding** and sunbathe while studying for their final exams in tiny tank tops and shorts."

"Guys at this school **are either immature or quiet**. The immature guys are the ones at the bars all up on every chick they see and throwing out their lines at you like those lines actually have ever worked on someone in the past. One time, I actually had a guy come up to me and say, 'Do you know karate?' I said, 'No, why?' and he goes, 'Cause your body's kickin'!'"

"The **girls are pretty hot**. They're all differently 'stacked.' The guys are cool and level-headed."

"It seems like the girls are hotter during the first and last months of school every year. They must hide behind sweaters or skip classes in the winter. The ones that are still out in the wintertime aren't disappointing; there's just **more to look at when it's warm** out."

The College Prowler Take On...
Guys & Girls

During the week, everyone's lust is dulled by classes, but on weekend nights, freshman and sophomore dorms, party houses, and bars overflow with sexual energy. A majority of freshmen seem to be sexually active. Most UB students "grow up," however, and get exclusive after freshman and sophomore year. Single upperclassmen complain that it's tough to find a hot guy or a pretty girl who's not in a relationship and who's not a jerk. In terms of looks, UB is a numbers game—there are thousands of hot guys and girls, but also, thousands of busted ones. Being easygoing is a virtue at UB; students who are perceived to be trying too hard are disliked.

UB's guy and girl scene is made up of different subcultures. Many guys and girls from upstate don't like Long Island girls, who have a reputation for being rich, rude, and promiscuous. They're known to talk on their cell phones in libraries and to wear tank-tops in January while whining about the weather in thick accents. Conversely, guys and girls from downstate often find upstate students to be plain and dull. UB has several classic types, including artsy girls who dress in fashionable outfits cobbled together from weekly trips to the thrift store, metrosexual guys who put lots of wax in their hair and try to look like models from mall stores, Italian guys from downstate who blare hip-hop from their SUVs and ooze with testosterone, and some international students who wear cheap sweaters and shirts buttoned all the way to the top. It's an exciting scene, and on weekend nights, everybody who wants some can get it.

B

The College Prowler® Grade on

Guys: B

A high grade for Guys indicates that the male population on campus is attractive, smart, friendly, and engaging, and that the school has a decent ratio of guys to girls.

B+

The College Prowler® Grade on

Girls: B+

A high grade for Girls not only implies that the women on campus are attractive, smart, friendly, and engaging, but also that there is a fair ratio of girls to guys.

Athletics

The Lowdown On... Athletics

Athletic Division:
NCAA Division I

Conference:
Mid-American Conference (MAC)

School Mascot:
Victor E. Bull, Victoria S. Bull

Males Playing Varsity Sports:
266 (3%)

Females Playing Varsity Sports:
210 (3%)

→

Men's Varsity Sports:

Baseball
Basketball
Cross-Country
Football
Soccer
Swimming
Tennis
Track & Field
Wrestling

Women's Varsity Sports:

Basketball
Crew
Cross-Country
Soccer
Softball
Swimming
Tennis
Track & Field
Volleyball

Club Sports:

Baseball (Men's)
Boxing (Men's, Women's)
Crew (Men's)
Cycling (Men's, Women's)
Drug-Free Power Lifting (Men's, Women's)
Field Hockey (Women's)
Gymnastics (Men's, Women's)
Ice Hockey (Men's, Women's)

(Club Sports, continued)

Judo/Ju Jutsu/Aikido (Men's, Women's)
Lacrosse (Men's, Women's)
Roller Hockey (Men's, Women's)
Rugby (Men's, Women's)
Seido Karate (Men's, Women's)
Ski Team (Men's, Women's)
Soccer (Men's, Women's)
Tae Kwon Do (Men's, Women's)
Tennis (Men's, Women's)
Ultimate Frisbee (Men's, Women's)
Volleyball (Men's)

Intramurals:

Badminton (Men's, Women's)
Basketball (Men's, Women's)
Flag Football (Men's, Women's)
Floor Hockey (Men's, Women's)
Racquetball (Men's, Women's)
Roller Hockey (Men's, Women's)
Soccer (Men's, Women's)
Softball (Men's, Women's)
Squash (Men's, Women's)
Tennis (Men's, Women's)
Volleyball (Men's, Women's)

Athletic Fields

UB Stadium, RAC Field (Soccer), Rotary Field, Ellicott Rugby Pitch

Getting Tickets

Students are admitted free to all sporting events. Except for the first home football game of the season or late-season basketball games when the team is hot, you'll never have trouble finding a seat.

Most Popular Sports

As it improves in conference play, the men's basketball team is starting to draw big crowds. The student section, also known as the Sea of Blue, is filled with vocal "Mighty Maniacs" (sponsored by Mighty Taco, a local Mexican food chain). After victories, everyone stands while the band plays the alma mater and the players run through the section giving the crowd high-fives. However, though Buffalo is a dyed-in-the-wool football town, the UB football team is consistently ranked among the worst in Division I-A. Though they draw nearly 10,000 fans per game, including a group of die-hards, most students respond to their losing ways with apathy or disdain. On the club sport side, UB has highly-ranked rugby and ultimate Frisbee teams. Students say the popular and well-organized intramural teams are a great way to meet people on campus.

Overlooked Teams

While UB's marquee sports have struggled, several sports—including the wrestling team and the men's and women's soccer teams—are very competitive in the MAC.

Best Place to Take a Walk

Amherst's popular jogging and cycling path runs through North Campus. Many students don't know that there are also paths in Letchworth Woods (near the Ellicott Complex dorms) and Walton Wood Park (off Audubon Parkway just north of campus). Delaware Park, Buffalo's magnificent public park, is a five-minute drive from South Campus.

Gyms/Facilities

Alumni Arena

According to the original campus plans, architects built cavernous Alumni Arena close to the academic buildings to encourage physical fitness among students. Yet, in the minds of workout purists, that strategy has worked too well. While Alumni's main weight room is large and well-appointed, it's crowded during weekdays; you'll probably have to wait for machines. Alumni also has seven racquetball courts, two squash courts, basketball courts, a dance studio, a spinning room, a jogging track, a sauna and steam room, and an Olympic-size pool that's often open for recreational use. Special facilities downstairs allow varsity athletes to avoid the teeming masses.

Ellicott Fields

Several athletic facilities are located in a field just east of the Ellicott Complex, including the University Tennis Club, basketball courts, handball courts, a soccer field, and a rugby pitch. In the warm months, the basketball courts are home to intense games, often among people who played street ball together in New York City.

Clark Hall (South Campus)

An old stone building that reeks of centuries of sweat, Clark Hall houses a gym, a swimming pool, a dance studio, racquetball courts, squash courts, a weight room, and a wrestling room. The boxing club practices in the basement. While Clark can't compare in size, some students prefer its intimacy to Alumni's stale modernity.

Students Speak Out On...
Athletics

"Varsity sports are something of a joke, but they're on their way to getting better. It's still a lot of fun to go to the games and cheer. Intramurals are pretty popular, as far as I can tell."

"Varsity sports are about **as popular as heat rash**. No more than a few thousand students ever attend the football games (except for the season opener, which is always packed), and more people attend the cross-dressing fashion show in the Student Union than the basketball games."

"Varsity sports would be big if the teams could put together some wins. The student body is **hungry for a good team**."

"Being a varsity athlete, I'd say that varsity sports are **big and, for the most part, successful**. Although our revenue-producing sports are inconsistent at times, the University definitely would not be the same without the athletic environment."

"Though the school tries to promote it, football doesn't get a lot of attention, generally due to the fact **that they lose a lot**. When the basketball team gets on a roll, Alumni Arena is a great place to catch a game. Lots of students take part in a wide variety of intramurals and club sports."

"The switch to Division I has sparked heated debates. The problems are too numerous to count. **We have the lowest attendance** in the Mid-American conference, even among losing teams. In truth, I have been to about a dozen football and basketball games in college. I don't mind watching a losing game, but I hate watching a game that's not even close. I'd rather go to Syracuse and watch a real team play."

"The men's basketball team always manages to put on a good game and is definitely **worth going to see** on every occasion possible. Almost any intramural sport you could want to play is offered, and they are always a lot of fun."

"The MAC is a solid conference for most sports, but **UB is not very competitive** in it. The men's and women's soccer teams always do fairly well. The track and cross-country teams have improved every year, but they still place in the middle of the pack at their respective conference meets. The men's basketball team seems to be improving each year, and this year, they are fighting for a home playoff game. Football attracts large crowds in the beginning of the year, but sometimes, only for high-budget halftime shows. As the weather gets colder and the team continually fails to win, crowds begin to diminish because all hopes for a decent season are gone."

"UB just moved up to Division I, and they have **yet to become competitive** or grow a fan base. It doesn't look like things are about to improve, either."

"Varsity sports are big on campus—at least when the teams are doing well. Unfortunately, **UB has fair-weather fans**. But usually there is at least one team doing well, so there's always something to cheer and paint our faces about. As can be expected, intramural and club sports are big to those who play them. Quite a few people do get involved in intramurals. I've been meaning to join a volleyball team myself."

"Varsity sports suck. Our teams suck. Intramural sports are more exciting to be a part of, as you compete against fellow teams of students. This is **definitely not a big sports town**, though."

"Varsity sports on campus are not that good and lack student popularity. Intramural sports have a good following, and there are **many to choose from**."

"UB is definitely not a school that lives and dies by its athletic teams. It's far from being a Duke or a Penn State, but Division I athletics are fewer than 10 years old for all sports. It takes a while to build a formidable reputation. Who knows what the future will hold, but for now, the only big news that spreads around campus is when the football team wins their only game of the season or **how low they are in the national rankings**."

The College Prowler Take On...
Athletics

In the early '90s, UB's athletic programs moved up to Division I after decades in Division III. Five years ago, the Bulls made another quick jump to the competitive Mid-American Conference, home to powerhouses like Marshall and Kent State. Despite huge levels of promotion (particularly for football), the teams have failed to inspire much of a following on campus. The hapless football team is so pathetic they are often ranked near the bottom of ESPN's "Bottom 10." Over 20,000 students usually come out for the home opener, but interest trails off as the losses mount. Some students genuinely hate the football team, and professors complain about it every day. They say the huge amounts of money that are invested in the program (each of the 100 players on the squad gets a full scholarship) could be better invested in academics.

But in the spring of 2004, the basketball team went on a tear and UB got a taste of the potential of big-time sports. Toward the end of the season, thousands of blue-clad "Mighty Maniacs" crowded like sweaty sardines in the large student section, cheering and chanting loudly for the entire game. The fans even rushed the court after a stunning home victory against Kent State (a top 30 team) and a first-round playoff win against Northern Illinois. The other sports teams have had mixed success—wrestling and women's soccer are both strong in their conferences, while tennis and baseball are weak. UB fields top-notch club teams, and many students also join intramural sports leagues which are generally taken more seriously at UB than at other schools.

B-

The College Prowler® Grade on

Athletics: B-

A high grade in Athletics indicates that students have school spirit, that sports programs are respected, that games are well-attended, and that intramurals are a prominent part of student life.

Nightlife

The Lowdown On... Nightlife

Club and Bar Prowler: Popular Nightlife Spots!

Club Crawler:

While Cloud 9, the only University Heights club, closed years ago, the downtown club scene remains lively. Buffalo has several clubs that cater to everyone from teenyboppers to the '80s nostalgia crowd, and there are also a handful of good live-music joints.

Club Marcella

622 Main St., Downtown

(716) 847-6850

www.clubmarcella.com

While Marcella is known around town as a gay club, it draws a few straight guys (and more than a few straight girls who come when they want to dance with people who really know how). It's pricey by Buffalo standards, but it offers a truly big-city atmosphere. Marcella's is a great scene, but it's not for everyone. Patrons should have an open mind and be willing to expect anything.

→

The Continental

212 Franklin St., Downtown

(716) 855-3938

If most Chippewa clubs hang with the popular crowd, the Continental is the Strip's ill-tempered and unapologetic gothic little brother. Nearly everyone acknowledges its legendary status. Johnny Rzeznik and the Goo Goo Dolls honed their style here in the '80s. The Continental is still known as a good live-music establishment, particularly for local punk bands and college bands on tour. If you're tempted by the underworld, and you've figured out how to dance to industrial rock, then the Continental is for you.

Mohawk Place

47 E Mohawk Pl., Downtown

(716) 855-3931

www.mohawkplace.com

Mohawk Place advertises itself as Buffalo's best live music club. This intimate little joint is just off the beaten path in downtown Buffalo. Local indie fans get excited about many of the bands that are booked here, though few register on the average college student's radar.

Nietzsche's

248 Allen St., Downtown

(716) 886-8539

www.nietzsches.com

(Nietzsche's, continued)

Along with Mohawk Place and the Showplace Theater, Buffalo music fans consider Nietzsche's one of the best venues for local bands. It's not a very big bar, but it has hosted some popular bands including Phish and 10,000 Maniacs. Drinks are a little more expensive than other bars, except on Saturday afternoons, when Nietzsche's offers $2 pints of Guinness and $1.50 mixed drinks.

Quote

236 Delaware Ave., Downtown

(716) 854-2853

www.westchippewa.com/quote.html

Both Quote and the clubbier Red Room a few doors down have become popular spots on Chippewa in the last few years. Both establishments have spacious, popular dance floors and cater to a younger crowd. Some purists find Quote and the Red Room to be too flashy and gimmicky for their tastes, but they're good places to party if you like top 40 music and you want to let loose. There are a lot of contests (often in conjunction with local radio stations), and you're likely to meet some campus celebrities. Quote is very popular with campus sororities, including the chapter featured on *Sorority Life 2*.

→

Utopia

228 Franklin St., Downtown

(716) 852-1164

www.westchippewa.com/utopia.html

This relatively big "club for everybody" is the first stop on Chippewa for many younger people in Buffalo's club crowd. It's got big, powerful speakers that send out a pulse-pounding bass, compelling everyone to dance (whether they're any good or not). Now that Cloud 9 in the Heights has closed, Utopia is the most popular destination for UB freshmen and sophomores; but some students complain about dull music, long lines, and the steep $10 under-21 cover charge.

Bar Prowler:

Allen Street Grill (a.k.a. the Old Pink, Two-Two-Three Allen, or the Pink Flamingo)

223 Allen St., Allentown

(716) 884-4338

The Old Pink is nestled in Allentown among tall trees, brownstones, art galleries, and used bookstores. It's got a unique scene that has earned it many "Buffalo's Best Kept Secret" honors (to the point that it's not much of a secret anymore). The décor is shabby and the floors are uneven, but it's an intimate, honest place; a good bar where you can spend quality time with your best friends.

(Allen Street, continued)

Real DJ's spin what many call Buffalo's best bar music. If you think the Heights is too played, Chippewa's too glitzy, Elmwood's too old, and Canada's irrelevant because you're 21, then you'll probably feel at home at the Pink.

Alternative Brews

3488 Sheridan Dr., Amherst

(716) 446-0424

www.alternativebrews.com

Most of the watering holes around North Campus are strictly neighborhood bars, and because students don't live in the real neighborhoods, they're not interested. But this inventive little tavern amid strip malls on Sheridan Drive attracts a younger crowd with its truly delicious homemade beers, including the popular Hazelnut Lager. One telling fact about Alternative Brews is you can't get pitchers. They're not in business to get people wasted. Because it's technically a cigar bar, Alternative Brews allows smoking (if you don't like the smell, you should stay away).

Drink Specials: Two-for-one well drinks during happy hour (4 p.m. to 7 p.m. weekdays)

→

→

Broadway Joe Bar

3051 Main St., University Heights

(716) 837-3650

www.bjoes.com

What more can you say about a place that was ranked the ninth best dive bar in the United States? Broadway Joe's in the Heights offers the strip's best live music practically every night of the week, including the popular Thursday night Baby Steps hip hop series. Indie Mondays feature upcoming rock bands that sometimes go on to dominate the regional scene. If you have a band and you're any good, there's a chance you can get your start at Broadway Joe's.

D'Arcy McGee's

257 Franklin St., Downtown

(716) 853-3600

www.westchippewa.com/darcy.html

D'Arcy's is part of a four-level entertainment complex on Franklin Street near the Chippewa Strip. It attracts an older, downtown crowd, particularly with its well-priced happy hour specials. The thickly-paneled first floor bar is surprisingly intimate, given its size. Bands play on the large patio through the winter. The D'Arcy's building also features Rhino Room, a mellow cigar bar on the second floor, and Skybar, a rooftop bar with a nice view of Chippewa's neon signs and madding crowds.

McMonkeez

69 W. Chippewa St., Downtown

(716) 853-5555

www.westchippewa.com/zoobar.html

This bar has the worst name in Buffalo. And while it's not outstanding in any way, McMonkeez is still a Chip Strip staple. Like many of the other downtown bars, McMonkeez has a great no-cover happy hour. It's also a little more laid-back than your average downtown meat market/bar, and it has a diverse clientele. The handsome and comfortable bar Barristers and the dance club Level are adjacent to McMonkeez.

Molly's Pub

3199 Main St., University Heights

(716) 836-6559

While Molly's might look modest from the exterior, this friendly two-level bar is packed to the gills on Thursday night, when they offer 25-cent drafts and $2.50 pitchers. On the other nights, it's quieter and more laid-back than the other Heights bars. Recently, the Friday night live music schedule featured popular local rock band More Than Me.

→

Mr. Goodbar

1110 Elmwood Ave., West Side

(716) 882-4000

Though it is located on the West Side close to Buff State, Goodbar is surprisingly popular with UB students. It's older than the Heights bars, and while nobody likes to admit it, it's more sophisticated, too. Goodbar draws an older crowd and offers a diverse entertainment lineup that ranges from rock to improv comedy. Most everyone agrees it's a good time, especially if you catch it on a busy night.

Drink specials: $5 pitchers and $2.25 bottles of Labatt Blue on Wednesdays

PJ Bottoms

3270 Main St., University Heights

(716) 833-3270

When you're a senior, the crazy stories you tell about going out as a freshman will probably be set at PJ's in the Heights. It's a crowded, loud, sloppy, drunk scene heavy on freshmen and sophomores. The most popular deal is the $3.50 Rolling Rock pitchers on Saturdays. It's a good bar to hook up at, but there's not much room to dance if you don't want to be groped. PJ's relatively strict dress code mandates sweaters or collared shirts and khakis.

The Shaker Lounge

220 Delaware Ave., Downtown

(716) 852-6200

This stylish, upscale bar is the only martini bar on the Chippewa Strip, and it's a classy departure from the run-down joints in the Heights. Located in the lobby of a pricey downtown hotel, Shaker Lounge attracts high-roller students who prefer quality over quantity when it comes to their drinks. Its signature drinks are the fruit-flavored martinis such as the Appletini (with sour apple vodka) and the Chocolate Covered Banana Martini. Shaker Lounge has a rotating specials menu from month to month.

The Steer

3151 Main St., University Heights

(716) 838-0478

Flaming tiki torches on the patio draw hundreds of students to the Steer on weekend nights. While each Heights bar has its fervent backers, the Steer—your average all-American college bar—is probably the most popular. It's the biggest and often the most crowded. Some criticize its clientele as frat kids and the "Abercrombie crowd," and the drinks are more expensive than the other Heights bars, but it's a good all-around place to go with your friends, whether you want to chill out or meet some guys or girls.

Third Base

3264 Main St., University Heights

(716) 833-1284

Once ranked one of the top college bars in the country, Third Base has calmed down in recent years and is now known as the Heights' "chill bar." There's a patio in the back and a nice pool table and dart boards in the front. Except for drunks who don't know any better, there's not much dancing. This is a great place to come on an off night with friends or on a night when you want to have fun without getting wasted.

Other Places to Check Out:

67 West

Anchor Bar

Barrel House

Barristers

Big Shotz

The Blu Room

Buffalo Wild Wings

Gabriel's Gate

Iberia

Lafayette Tap Room

Level

The Red Room

Soho

Yank's

Useful Resources for Nightlife:

Artvoice (Buffalo's alternative newspaper), the *Beast* (a weekly humor publication with an irreverent and hilarious bar guide)

Bars Close At:

4 a.m.

Primary Areas with Nightlife:

Allentown

The Chippewa Strip

The Elmwood Strip

Niagara Falls, Canada

University Heights

Cheapest Place to Get a Drink:
Molly's Pub in the Heights

Student Favorites:
Alternative Brews
Broadway Joe's
PJ Bottoms
The Steer

Favorite Drinking Games:
Beer Pong/Beirut
Century Club
Mafia
Power Hour
Quarters

What to Do if You're Not 21

Many younger students go where the drinking age is 19: bars and strip clubs in Canada. Clifton Hill in Niagara Falls is the Las Vegas of the North. It's a neon-lit tourist trap, complete with a wax museum and a popular casino. Often students will drive up there, go to the casino, get trashed in the bars, and then spend the night at a cheap Clifton Hill hotel. The best Niagara Falls bars and clubs are listed below.

If you want to stay local and legal, many clubs are 18-and-over all the time; you just have to be 21 to drink. Try Utopia, Club Marcella, or the Continental downtown.

The Daily Planet

4573 Queen St., Niagara Falls, Canada

(905) 371-1722

Located in a residential neighborhood five minutes from the Clifton Hill district, Daily Planet is the biggest and nicest bar in Niagara Falls. It has several rooms, including a VIP level. The bar is spacious and well-lit, the brews are always ice cold, and there are big, inviting booths. Don't forget, though, that the Niagara Falls bars close at 2 a.m., a full two hours earlier than Buffalo bars.

Rumours

4960 Clifton Hill, Niagara Falls, Canada

(905) 358-6152

This Canadian dance club rivals or surpasses the Chippewa Street clubs. It's a great place to go in the summer when it's open a full seven days a week. Rumours (spelled with a "u," the Canadian way) is situated right in the middle of the neon-splashed Clifton Hill strip. Laser effects light up the spacious main room, which has a huge dance floor.

The Wild Mushroom

5633 Victoria Ave., Niagara Falls, Canada

(905) 357-2788

It's still tacky in a classic Niagara Falls way, but for many of the mellower types in UB's Canada crowd, the Mushroom is a nice departure from the abject glitz on the rest of Clifton Hill. There's a pool table, a dart board (dangerously close to the door), and many large television screens that always seem to be playing hockey highlights. The drinks are good but generally more expensive than in the Heights, even considering that they are in Canadian dollars.

Local Specialties

Buffalo once had a proud brewing tradition, but it died years ago along with our grain-milling tradition and steelmaking tradition. Because Canada is just across the Niagara River, Canadian beers such as Molson and Labatt are especially popular around town. Nobody drinks Genesee, despite the fact that it is brewed in nearby Rochester.

Organization Parties

Many of the nearly 3,000 students and faculty who are members of the UB ski club Schussmeisters gather for a massive members-only party at a local ski resort in February. Otherwise, official club parties are few and far between; organizations prefer to have unofficial events off campus.

Frats

See the Greek section!

Students Speak Out On...
Nightlife

"The parties in University Heights are basically all the same: $5 cover at a big house with a keg or two in the basement, while rap and R&B that was popular three years ago blasts from various speakers."

"Parties on campus are generally not open-door parties, so the on-campus party situation is **generally based on who you know**. As for off-campus parties, on a Friday or Saturday, you can generally find a party to crash somewhere in University Heights."

"The house parties in University Heights are the best parties, as long as the police don't feel inclined to leave their permanent coffee break at the Mobil station. The big parties can have hundreds of people, and in nice weather, it's possible to walk through the Heights and **see a dozen parties going on**."

"Molly's is the place to be **Thursday nights for cheap drinks**, the Steer is where to go for the preppy kids, Broadway Joe's is the place for live music, and PJ Bottoms is where to go to hit on local high school girls who get in with notes from their parents."

"You have two failsafe options for nighttime entertainment: Chippewa and the Heights. Chippewa-goers are still looking around for the cameras that followed the *Sorority Life* kids around. The Heights-dwellers **don't give a crap**."

"On Main Street, you have PJ Bottoms, which you have to experience if you go to UB, but mostly freshmen attend this brothel. Another bar that is a good time is the Steer, but **be ready to bump elbows on the weekend and pay some serious cash**, due to the lack of specials. Down on Chippewa, you have too many to name. Come down here, and you won't look any further for a good time."

"**Downtown Buffalo is the best location**. There are a lot of fun places to go where you can get all dressed up and go dancing. This is a good change of pace from the Main Street bar scene. For a more laid-back situation, where you can sit and have a beer with your buddy, Elmwood is the place to go. Other than that, there are a lot of independent bars you can go to, depending on what your mood is."

"The best bars are **located in Allentown**. They're a little dirty, but they have the best music, cheapest prices, and friendliest clientele. The Old Pink, actually called the Allen Street Grill, though it acquired its nickname because it was once called the Pink Flamingo, is absolutely the essence of Buffalo. The Old Pink doesn't apologize for itself. It's honest. It's come as you are. The floor is uneven, but the beer is cold, the people are loud, and the tunes are a gritty mix of current rock and roll and the classics that helped shape today's music."

"Parties on campus are non-existent. But just cross the street from South Campus **any weekend night and pick your poison**: the frat party, the crew-team party, the all-male a cappella group party, the vegan anarchist party, or the 'dress like an '80s pop-star' party."

"House parties that involve alcohol and socializing generally draw a white crowd, while the parties with loud reggae music blaring and couples wall-to-wall dancing, sweating, and loving it draw a predominantly black crowd. The bars and clubs on Main Street are an attraction from Thursday to Saturday night. The **clubs downtown are hot spots** for after parties, reggae and hip hop parties, and hot guest performers. Partying is a word to which all young people relate."

"Go to frat parties. Anybody can score, as long as they keep their **standards low and their spirits high**."

"Generally, Chippewa is the best place to go out to the bars. There are also bars around South Campus, but I don't like any of them. **House parties on weekends** are the norm. My personal favorite bar is the Barrel House on Chippewa Street."

"Frat parties, such as they are at UB, are a rite of passage. While it's warm out, they're a blast. Everyone **hangs out in the backyard** of a skuzzy Heights house (behind a blue tarp, so the cops can't see you, as if they didn't know what you were doing) and tries to get a red cup full of Beast or whatever cheap, watery beer they're serving. By sophomore year, the hype has died down, and most people move on to barhopping. Main Street is kind of like Playskool's 'My First Bar' area."

The College Prowler Take On... Nightlife

Buffalo is a great college party town. There are martini bars for high-rollers, chill bars for old friends, live-music joints for the emo and hardcore crowd, freshmen bars where lecherous seniors can hook up with freshmen girls, and plenty of clubs for people who want to go, well, clubbing. Canada, where the drinking age is 19, is just a few miles away. Hard drinks are cheap, and covers are either low or non-existent. Bartenders are friendly, wise, and liberal with free drinks. Cold Canadian beer is cheap and always on tap. And if you weren't having enough fun already, the bars are open until 4 a.m., two hours later than most everywhere else in the United States.

Most UB students start out by going in the Heights to house parties and any of Main Street's seven bars. On warm nights, you can walk down any street and pass dozens of parties. Students usually pre-game in their dorms, apartments, or houses and then head for the bars. After a year or two of the Heights scene, students venture downtown to the Chippewa Strip or head over to the Westside and get to know the many fine bars in the Elmwood Village and Allentown districts. Many students who are underage go to Niagara Falls, Canada, where friends often throw in $5 or $10 each, get a cheap hotel room on Clifton Hill, and party all night. Parties on campus are pretty rare, however, because police are strict and dorm rooms are relatively small. Still, students in the top floors of the Ellicott towers have been known to hold parties where there are different drinks in every room.

A

The College Prowler® Grade on

Nightlife: A

A high grade in Nightlife indicates that there are many bars and clubs in the area that are easily accessible and affordable. Other determining factors include the number of options for the under-21 crowd and the prevalence of house parties.

Greek Life

The Lowdown On... Greek Life

Number of Fraternities:
11

Number of Sororities:
11

Undergrad Men in Fraternities:
2%

Undergrad Women in Sororities:
1%

Fraternities on Campus:

Alpha Sigma Phi
Delta Omega Psi
Lambda Upsilon Lambda
Phi Kappa Psi
Phi Kappa Theta
Pi Lambda Phi
Sigma Beta Rho
Sigma Chi Omega
Sigma Phi Epsilon
Sigma Pi
Theta Delta Sigma

Sororities on Campus:

Alpha Epsilon Phi
Alpha Gamma Delta
Alpha Phi
Delta Xi Omega
Kappa Phi Epsilon
Lambda Pi Upsilon
Omega Phi Beta
Sigma Delta Tau
Sigma Lambda Gamma
Xi Delta Phi
Zeta Phi Beta

Multicultural Colonies:

Alpha Kappa Delta Phi
Delta Sigma Theta
Kappa Phi Lambda
Lamba Phi Delta
Lambda Phi Epsilon
Lambda Theta Alpha
Nu Alpha Phi
Phi Iota Alpha
Pi Delta Psi
Sigma Psi Zeta

Other Greek Organizations:

Greek Council
Greek Peer Advisors
Interfraternity Council
Order of Omega
Panhellenic Council

Did You Know?

UB's chapter of the Delta Xi Omega sorority and the Sigma Chi Omega fraternity **were featured on MTV's *Sorority Life 2* and *Fraternity Life*** in the spring of 2003. Mostly everyone at UB watched the show. Students enjoyed the spectacle of the production. Cameras followed the kids all over campus and the Heights in the fall.

Students Speak Out On...
Greek Life

"Greek life is almost nonexistent; at least for me it's been. I know a bunch of people who have pledged, but I haven't really felt the influence at all."

"After the boom from MTV's *Sorority Life 2* and *Fraternity Life*, it seems like the world thinks UB is a Greek school. We're not. In fact, I don't think I could name three Greek organizations by name. Greek-letter organizations are **tight and cliquey**, and they stick together, which is, I suppose, their definition."

"I hate the Greeks. They are a bunch of **rich, pompous, arrogant pains**. The frats suck, the sororities suck, and they are not even worth considering."

"I can give my opinion on Greek life from the African American perspective. I used to think Greek life was nothing but organized cliques. But when I go to an event and they have that section where all the Greeks give their frat/sorority call and do their stroll, I get a little envious. Those kids are so full of **pride for their organizations**. Greek life might not be for me, but it is for many students at UB. Whether you hate it or love it, everyone can acknowledge that Greek life is a substantial part of UB's student life."

"Don't let MTV fool you—Greek life is **just about nonexistent** at UB. The only places where fraternity or sorority culture even exists are at Bert's, the Steer, and the tables in the Student Union."

"Greek life is **big if you're into it**. If you're not, there are plenty of other clubs and groups of kids to hang out with. The school is only something like five percent Greek. You can go to their parties for a measly $5 and get all-you-can-drink beer. Not a bad deal."

"**Greek life at UB is stupid**. What's the point? Oh yeah, fraternizing with your 'brothers' as you haze each other in a latently homosexual fashion."

"Only **a very small percentage of students** decide to pledge fraternities and sororities. Neither are very visible on campus.'"

The College Prowler Take On...
Greek Life

The filming of MTV's *Sorority Life 2* and *Fraternity Life* at UB in the fall of 2002 was a major event on campus. When the show aired the following spring, students gathered at their friends' houses to watch Buffalo on national television. Statistics showed that the school's home page got three times as many hits as usual while the show aired, and the Office of Admissions received thousands more applications. But everyone from Buffalo who watched the show knew the irony. UB is just not a big Greek school.

Still, most students would be shocked to hear that only two percent of UB guys and one percent of girls go Greek. While the Greeks are generally ridiculed, most students acknowledge that they have a more considerable role on campus than their numbers indicate. One reason for this is that many frats and sororities exist off the books. Because UB has draconian drinking and hazing policies for Greek organizations (that prohibit road trips, open parties, and Greek-letter apparel, among other things), many groups were barred years ago, but continue to induct members, throw parties, and nail their Greek letters to their upstairs balconies in the Heights. Frats and sororities are also very visible in the Student Union, where their pledges stake-out the biggest and best tables early in the morning. And while most students mock the Greeks, many of those students also frequent popular frat and sorority parties, particularly in the early fall and late spring. UB's relatively weak fraternity and sorority scene is a product of the decentralized campus, not a lack of enthusiasm for partying hard.

C-

The College Prowler® Grade on

Greek Life: C-

A high grade in Greek Life indicates that sororities and fraternities are not only present, but also active on campus. Other determining factors include the variety of houses available and the respect the Greek community receives from the rest of the campus.

Drug Scene

The Lowdown On...
Drug Scene

Most Prevalent Drugs on Campus:

Alcohol
Caffeine
Ecstasy
Marijuana
Psychedelic Mushrooms

Liquor-Related Referrals:

156

Liquor-Related Arrests:

26

Drug-Related Referrals:

78

Drug-Related Arrests:

4

Drug Counseling Programs

Student Wellness Team Counseling Services

(716) 645-2720

Services: Online mental health screening, group counseling, individual counseling, crisis intervention, safe zone, self-help materials

Students Speak Out On...
Drug Scene

"If you are not interested in drugs, they're easy to stay away from. If you are interested in drugs, they're easy to find."

"The drug scene is **mostly hippies on pot** and yuppies on coke. Go, frats, go!"

"The drug scene on campus is much **like any other college**. Kids smoke 'the pot.' Some kids do more. Basically, drugs are almost always available if you look hard enough, much like any other college. Punishment for getting caught depends on the kid and on the punisher. I got caught smoking my freshman year and got 30 hours of community service. Other kids I know got 200."

"Are there college students at UB? Well, then there will be drugs and alcohol. **I'm sure anyone can find drugs** if they're looking for them, but I've never been interested, and no one has ever approached me with illegal drugs of any kind."

"While it is definitely possible to get harder drugs like cocaine and ecstasy (mostly through sororities and seedy fraternities) around campus, softer drugs like marijuana and 'shrooms dominate the student population. Though there are periodic dry spells, UB's proximity to **Canada makes it easy to find pot** at fair prices with little hassle."

"**Pot is pretty popular**, along with alcohol, but I think that's true at every college campus."

"I try to avoid the drug scene, for the most part. However, **there is a lot of pot use**, and I'm sure there are harder drugs that are widely used by the student population."

"Drugs, like most bad things in this world, happen everywhere, usually when you're not looking. They range from not so bad to really, really bad. I gather most of the really serious narcotics use was already in place before most of the users came to Buffalo—but we live in a city; **it's going to be rampant**."

"UB has drugs, but they are **not very prevalent on campus**. You find your pot-heads here and there, but the harder drugs are behind closed doors. I would say drug use other than weed is pretty low. However, alcohol flows like water."

"It's fairly common to end up with a stoner in your hall in the dorms, but that is about the extent of drug use. **Most drug use here is recreational**."

The College Prowler Take On...
Drug Scene

The drug scene at UB is much like the student club scene. While it's easy to ignore if you don't want to get involved, there are plenty of opportunities for the enterprising student. Smoking pot in the dorms is common but risky because students can get community service hours from the student judiciary. The drug scene is more visible off campus. The majority of students don't try anything more serious than pot, but nobody has any illusions that more serious abuses don't happen behind closed doors. In recent years, ecstasy (or "E") has become popular at parties and clubs. Some students use 'shrooms, and there are plenty of rumors about cocaine use.

Partly due to traffic in potent Canadian pot, the city of Buffalo is an infamous transfer point in the international drug trade. As a result, though it exists almost completely below the radar of the campus culture, UB has a bizarre drug-trafficking underworld that only surfaces once or twice a semester when students hear of an armed robbery or kidnapping on campus. These incidents are extremely rare, however. While caffeine abuse plagues many colleges, it is not much of a factor at UB, partly because there are fewer academic pressures. But alcohol flows like Niagara Falls. The good news is that the school's diversity indicates that it's not the least bit difficult for a straight-edge student to find other people who want to have fun without getting wasted.

B+

The College Prowler® Grade on

Drug Scene: B+

A high grade in the Drug Scene indicates that drugs are not a noticeable part of campus life; drug use is not visible, and no pressure to use them seems to exist.

Campus Strictness

The Lowdown On...
Campus Strictness

What Are You Most Likely to Get Caught Doing on Campus?

- Breaking minor traffic rules
- Drinking underage
- Driving under the influence
- Hosting a party where people are drinking underage
- Parking illegally
- Possessing marijuana in the dorms

Students Speak Out On...
Campus Strictness

"Campus police will bust you if you are stupid about it. Same with most of the RAs. As long as you don't get stupid, you will be fine."

"The **police are always serious**. RAs are usually much less serious and much more lenient, but it depends."

"Campus police are so-so, depending on whether or not you hit them on a good night. Usually they will write you up **only if you do something dumb** or if you have numerous complaints against you."

"On campus, **it's fairly easy to avoid trouble as long as you keep the party in your room** and don't cause problems. About the only people who actually get in trouble with campus police are the ones who get drunk and end up running around the dorms causing trouble."

"Campus police are strict about everything. Someone is always getting **arrested or hassled** about one thing or another—'one thing' meaning alcohol and 'another' meaning loud parties."

"I think there is **some racial profiling**. Most of my black, male friends have been stopped on campus while doing nothing more than walking to their dorms. I never hear my white friends complain about this. So, while the police do a decent job of keeping our campus safe, they could do well with some lessons in progressive thinking."

"I've never seen a campus police officer care about anything more than they do about double-parking. They're certainly all around town, but **they don't do much, as far as I can tell**. I still owe $30,538,593 on parking violations, though."

"Police normally leave you alone if you're good. An RA will come knocking on your door if you're too loud. They are fellow students, though, so most of them are cool and usually just ask you to keep it down. As long as you're not harvesting illegal drugs, you can pretty much **do whatever you want in your room**."

"I don't know how strict the police are. **I don't think I've ever talked to them**."

The College Prowler Take On...
Campus Strictness

For the most part, campus police officers are polite and professional. However, UB has an irreverent student body, so the police force is very unpopular. Students gripe whenever police interfere with their "right to break the law." The campus police force is relatively large and visible, although they don't usually have much to do on North Campus besides providing security for campus events and patrolling the loop roads. They were once famous for giving speeding tickets, but their citation books were taken last year, so they can't write moving violations anymore. Police are serious about ticketing illegally parked cars, however.

If they get along well with their RAs, students can get away with drinking in their dorm rooms without a problem. A few of the tougher RAs will write you up for public drunkenness. Smoking pot is another matter. Most get community service hours, but students who sell or have a big stash can be kicked out of school. The apartment complexes' rules about partying and underage drinking are also enforced surprisingly well. The strictness of police on campus just forces students to party off campus, where Buffalo cops are pretty lax. Police bust up Heights parties only if they get really loud and spill into the street; the general rule is that if you keep it in the back, they'll look the other way. But Amherst police are extremely tough. They take Amherst's ranking as "Safest U.S. Town" seriously, and they don't want anyone stepping out of line. Stick to the speed limit on Niagara Falls Boulevard and Millersport Highway, and don't follow too close, swear too loudly, or smile too broadly.

B

The College Prowler® Grade on

Campus Strictness: B

A high Campus Strictness grade implies an overall lenient atmosphere; police and RAs are fairly tolerant, and the administration's rules are flexible.

Parking

The Lowdown On... Parking

Approximate Parking Permit Cost:
None

UB Parking Services:
(716) 645-2516
ubparking@buffalo.edu
www.student-affairs.buffalo.edu/parking

Student Parking Lot?
Yes

Freshmen Allowed to Park?
Yes

Common Parking Tickets:
Expired Meter: $20
No Parking Zone: $20
Handicapped Zone: $50
Fire Lane: $20

Parking Permits

Parking permits for UB lots are free to all students.

Did You Know?

Best Places to Find a Parking Spot

- Arena Lot (North Campus)
- Center for Tomorrow Lot (North Campus)
- Cooke B Lot, Governors E Lot (North Campus)
- Lake LaSalle Lot (North Campus)
- Main-Bailey Lot (South Campus)
- Slee A Lot (North Campus)
- Special Events Lot (North Campus)
- Stadium Lot (North Campus)

Good Luck Getting a Parking Spot Here!

- Baird B Lot (North Campus)
- Diefendorf Lot (South Campus)
- Farber Lot (South Campus)
- Fronczak B Lot (North Campus)
- Jacobs A, B, and C Lots (North Campus)
- Ketter Lot (North Campus)
- Slee B Lot (North Campus)

Students Speak Out On...
Parking

"If there's one thing everyone agrees on at UB, it's that the parking is horrible. You often have to park far away from where you are going and take a long walk or ride a shuttle."

"**Parking on both campuses is abysmal**. Not only are the lots far from where you need to go, they are all way too small. Finding a parking spot is largely a matter of patient searching or simply being in the right place at the right time."

"It depends on the time of day. If you are showing up for a noon class during the week, expect to have to spend some time finding a spot and taking a hike across campus to your class. Everybody complains about parking, but that's because they try to show up two minutes before their class starts, and they're upset they can't get a spot right near the building. **Showing up early and expecting to walk** is key."

"**Parking is bad**. Just when you've done your job as a parking shark and stalked some unsuspecting guy from the building all the way to his car, some other toothless mongrel zooms in front of you, takes that spot you worked so hard for, and flips you off at the same time."

"Parking is horrible. Most of the time, **people will steal your spot** because they are ruthless, so take someone else's spot if you have to."

"Don't get me started. It's really the **worst aspect of student life**. On one hand, I'd rather not have multi-level parking garages that interrupt the luscious greenery our campus is proudly framed by. But I also don't want to have to do calf warm-ups every time I get out of my car and head through the tundra to class, which is on the other side of eternity."

"It's atrocious. There are no spots; at least, **none that are relatively close**. You can park at the Center for Tomorrow on the outskirts of campus and take a shuttle to the academic buildings, but that's no good if you're already three minutes late for your 9 a.m. class."

"Parking can be a challenge and very frustrating on certain days, and on other days, you can just pull into a spot. It's best just to **pick one parking lot and wait** for a spot to open up—if you have 15 minutes to wander the lot, you can always be at class on time."

"While parking is not the best situation, it could be a lot worse than it is. You can always park in the lots that feel like they're **10 miles away from your class** and take a shuttle to the Spine. I've never done it, but it's a good backup if necessary."

"Parking got so bad that the University commissioned a company to do a study of parking a few years ago. They came back and said that there are enough spots, just not enough close ones. Park at the Center for Tomorrow, they said. Take the shuttle, they recommend. They said you shouldn't circle the lots for an empty spot. **I say circle the lots**, and stalk people who are headed to their cars. It may not be the most polite thing to do, but I'm parking close, while Mr. Nice Guy is parking at the Center for Tomorrow."

"Parking can be a little rough. Add **10 minutes to when you need to leave for class**. After a few weeks, you'll figure out what to do."

"Parking is a pain. Commuters who have 8 a.m. classes will have no problem finding any space they want, but after 9:30 a.m., it's almost impossible to find a space near popular classroom buildings. Having to walk is something that just has to be dealt with, because **even the closest spots require some walking**. Parking in the winter is a disaster. No one can see the lines that assign spaces, so people just park freestyle."

The College Prowler Take On...
Parking

If you look under "bad (adj.)" in Roget's Thesaurus, you will find a number of words that have one thing in common: they all have been used to describe the parking situation at UB. Most students feel that UB's parking problems are a serious quality-of-life issue. And parking affects nearly everybody, because 20,000 students commute to campus, and most of the students in the dorms have a car parked in one of the lots. The good thing is that parking permits are free. And unlike many schools, there is always a spot somewhere on campus. Unfortunately, unless you arrive before 9:30 a.m. or after 2:30 p.m., you're probably going to have to walk nearly 10 minutes to get to your class.

William Greiner, who stepped down as president of UB in 2003, used to say "We don't have a parking problem; we have a walking problem." He caught a lot of heat for it. Instead of parking at a lot that's a bit further out, many drivers stalk students as they walk through the lots back to their cars. Once the departing student pulls out, battles sometimes ensue between two cars vying for that spot. Sometimes, middle fingers are exchanged. The smartest thing to do to avoid this ugly scenario is to learn the campus shuttle schedule, park in an outer lot, and take the shuttle to your building. Some upperclassmen have a favorite illegal spot close to the Spine where they swear they've never received a ticket. While a good find can work for a few months, everybody's luck cools eventually, because the campus police are serious about ticketing.

C

The College Prowler® Grade on

Parking: C

A high grade in this section indicates that parking is both available and affordable, and that parking enforcement isn't overly severe.

Transportation

The Lowdown On... Transportation

Ways to Get Around Town:

On Campus

UB Stampede

On North Campus, buses stop at Flint Loop, South Lake Village, Flint Village, Hadley Village, Flickinger Court, Governors, Lee Loop, and Ellicott. On South Campus, the stops are Goodyear, Main Circle, and Main-Bailey. Buses run approximately every 5–10 minutes during the academic year (and every 30–60 minutes during the summer).

Public Transportation

Niagara Frontier Transportation Authority (NFTA), (716) 855-7211

Taxi Cabs

Broadway Taxi, (716) 896-4600

Dependable Cab Co., (716) 876-5555

Liberty Cab Co., (716) 877-7111 or (800) 455-TAXI

→

Car Rentals

Alamo, local: (412) 472-5060
national: (800) 327-9633
www.alamo.com

Avis, local: (412) 472-5200
national: (800) 831-2847
www.avis.com

Budget, local: (412) 472-5252
national: (800) 527-0700
www.budget.com

Dollar, local: (412) 472-5100
national: (800) 800-4000
www.dollar.com

Enterprise,
local: (412) 472-3490
national: (800) 736-8222
www.enterprise.com

Hertz, local: (412) 472-5955
national: (800) 654-3131
www.hertz.com

National, local: (412) 472-5094
national: (800) 227-7368
www.nationalcar.com

Best Ways to Get Around Town

Drive

Bike – in the warm months

Take campus bus to Metro Bus or Metro Rail

Ways to Get Out of Town:

Airlines Serving Buffalo

AirTran, (800) 247-8726
www.airtran.com

American Airlines,
(800) 433-7300
www.aa.com

(Airlines, continued)

Continental, (800) 523-3273
www.continental.com

Comair, (800) 221-1212
www.comair.com

JetBlue, (800) 538-2583
www.jetblue.com

Northwest, (800) 225-2525
www.nwa.com

Southwest, (800) 435-9792
www.southwest.com

United, (800) 241-6522
www.united.com

US Airways, (800) 428-4322
www.usairways.com

Airport

Buffalo Niagara
International Airport

(716) 630-6000

The Buffalo Niagara International Airport is 7 miles and 15 minutes driving time from North Campus and South Campus.

How to Get to the Airport

The airport is close enough that your best bet is to ask a friend to drop you off. But if you don't mind a long bus ride, the NFTA's 30-Kenmore bus runs to the airport about every 90 minutes. It leaves from the lower bus loop at University Station on South Campus (check *www.nfta.com* for schedules). Airport Taxi Service/ITA Shuttle, (800) 551-9369, also takes students to the airport. A cab ride to the airport costs about $20.

Greyhound

Intercity buses stop at NFTA Terminal in downtown Buffalo, a 20-minute drive from North Campus and a 15-minute drive or subway ride from South Campus. For schedule information, call (800) 229-9424 or visit *www.greyhound.com*.

NFTA Terminal

181 Ellicott St.

Buffalo, NY 14203

(716) 855-7531

Amtrak

Two Amtrak stations serve Buffalo—a small station in suburban Depew and an even smaller station in downtown Buffalo.

Buffalo-Depew Station
55 Dick Rd.
Depew, NY 14043

Buffalo-Exchange Street Station
Exchange and Ellicott Streets
Buffalo, NY 14203

Travel Agents

AAA Travel
2658 Delaware Ave., Buffalo
(716) 873-0111

Elliott Travel Agency
2680 Delaware Ave., Buffalo
(716) 874-5700

Liberty Travel
3140 Sheridan Dr., Amherst
(716) 837-2222

The Travel Team
2495 Main St., Buffalo
(716) 862-7600

Students Speak Out On...
Transportation

"Transportation is all right. It depends where you're going. From Lee Loop to Ellicott, it is very good. The Governors stop can be inconsistent, and the same for the South Campus shuttle."

"Transportation on campus was **always a great resource**, and now with shuttle buses added to the mix it is even better. The only problem is the bus that runs between North Campus and South Campus. On weekends, everyone likes to go out to the bars near South Campus. The bars don't close until 4 a.m., but the bus stops running by 2 a.m. All North Campus residents are deprived of two hours of fun if the bus is their only means of transportation back to the dorms."

"Public transportation here, I thought, was really good after listening to friends from home talk about their schools. There are a lot of different buses for different purposes. There are tons of shuttles running all over North Campus very frequently. **Occasionally, there is a bus that goes to the mall, which is really convenient**."

"The subway is great if you want to go either downtown or to campus. Other than that, it's fairly useless, but then again, most places you want to go are either downtown or on campus. There's a shuttle on campus that runs to **almost every location at UB**, and occasionally, to the nearby mall. To get to some of the further spots out—like the Elmwood Avenue area, home of great retail shops and restaurants—you need either a car, a friend with a car, or a lot of cab money."

"**Taxis are fairly priced and easy to find around South Campus**. If you have to go downtown, I would recommend driving, because the narrow one-line 'subway system' is pretty pathetic."

"UB offers transportation **from almost anywhere to almost anywhere**. During the day on weekends, the bus and the shuttles run often, but there is often a long wait at non-peak times."

"It depends on the time of day. During the day, the busing on each campus and between campuses is great. But, though the buses run in the evening and nighttime hours, **don't count on being able to easily catch one**."

"Shuttles can bring you **around to the whole campus**. Getting to other places off campus is a little difficult if you don't have a car. If you want an off-campus job, you basically need a car, unless you start dating the fat chick down the hall that does have a car."

"If there is one thing at the top of a list of UB's good qualities, it is the transportation system around campus. There are a ton of buses that go **back and forth between the two campuses**. Once on either campus, the system is very efficient—shuttles have frequent stops all around the campus. My freshman year I was on crutches, and the transportation system was great at getting me around the campus."

"Between the bus systems, public transportation is pretty **easy to find**, and they also connect to the subway."

"The South Campus bus, although it gets crowded, is a really good method for **getting down to the bars on Main Street** so you don't have to worry about getting a designated driver or calling a cab. Another really convenient method of transportation is the subway, which runs directly from South Campus to downtown. Driving and parking downtown can be confusing anyway, so taking the subway is always a good method. The only problem is that it stops running really early (around midnight or 1 a.m.), which can be constricting."

The College Prowler Take On...
Transportation

Students who needed public transit between campuses used to be at the mercy of the Blue Birds, clattering blue buses held together with duct tape and chalked with graffitied statements like, "Out of Vietnam Now," or "Ronald Reagan: Four More Years!" However, in the past few years, the old Birds have been replaced by a shiny fleet of white buses. UB has also purchased a small army of shuttle vans that travel on different color-coded routes (Red, Orange, Green, Blue) within the campuses. Buffalo's light-rail line terminates at University Station on South Campus. While the little subway is somewhat of an urban joke in Buffalo, it's clean and well-used (if not by students). But UB has finally accepted that a long-rumored light-rail link to North Campus will probably never be built.

Everyone is happy with the inter-campus bus service during the day when buses run about every five minutes. Night and weekend service is less frequent. Buses are usually separated by 20–30-minute intervals. On weekend nights, the inter-campus bus becomes the fabled "drunk bus," which stops running just after 2 a.m. More and more students are using the shuttle vans to get from their apartment complexes or parking spots to the Spine. The subway is actually a popular way to get downtown for an event at Shea's (the major performance theater) or HSBC Arena (home of the Sabres and big concerts). Of course, the most popular way of getting around Buffalo is by car. There's a lot of parking everywhere, and you can get anywhere in the city (including the airport) in 15 to 20 minutes.

A-

The College Prowler® Grade on

Transportation: A-

A high grade for Transportation indicates that campus buses, public buses, cabs, and rental cars are readily-available and affordable. Other determining factors include proximity to an airport and the necessity of transportation.

Weather

The Lowdown On... Weather

Average Temperature:

Fall:	51 °F
Winter:	26 °F
Spring:	45 °F
Summer:	68 °F

Average Precipitation:

Fall:	3.65 in.
Winter:	3.13 in.
Spring:	3.13 in.
Summer:	3.61 in.

Students Speak Out On... Weather

"Buffalo has the absolute worst possible combination of wind and freezing temperatures. I can recall some times when the wind was so harsh you could not walk up hills because you were blown backwards."

"Everyone enjoys the season's first snowfall and a white Christmas, but unfortunately, those aren't the only two days it snows in Buffalo. Unless you are a fan of the winter, **the weather at UB sucks**. There is consistently warm weather for about a total of 10 weeks over the whole school year. There are always random days when it will be 60 in December, and everyone will sport their favorite summer attire that day, but overall, I'm not a fan of the winter."

"The weather ranges from extremely cold to tundra-like in the winter. Invest in a warm jacket, thermal gloves, five scarves, and a good pair of boots. **When it turns about 50 degrees out, people start wearing shorts**. By May, it's beautiful, and it stays that way until about September. The summers make it worth dealing with a little frostbite and a few feet of snow."

"One word: **sweaters**!"

"People who complain are just wusses. Get over it! If you don't like the cold, **quit complaining and move to Florida**."

"Cold. **Bitter and cold, except for the summertime**. And if you bring your little umbrella and your crazy handbag, you can fly away like Mary Poppins in the wind tunnel between the Promenade and Clemens Hall."

"The weather in Buffalo is the worst of anywhere in the world. It snows all the time. The sun disappears between late October and late April. Dress warm—**it is always cold**. You cannot pack too many sweaters. You will not want to go outside, ever. In short, the weather makes Buffalo a much worse place to live than it should be."

"There can be snow on the ground **over half the academic year**. If you love snow, Buffalo's the place to be. If you want to stay away from the snow, then you will enjoy that all of the academic buildings are connected by enclosed bridges, so you can walk from one class to another without going outside."

"**Bring three coats**: one for the below zero days, one for the high 20s days, and one for the days when Old Man Winter's hold is waning and the temperature climbs into the 50s. For the love of all that is good, please don't break out the shorts until it is at least 60 degrees. And even if you've done a bit of pre-gaming and feel like you have the fire inside, don't walk down to the Main Street bars in a tank top when it is 10 degrees outside. Warm is always more attractive than dead."

"Personally, I don't think the weather is **nearly as bad as everyone makes it out to be**. Usually, the problem is more the wind than the cold. I think you get used to it—although I know many others would disagree. Either way, remember your knit hat and gloves."

"The weather is very cold. Very cold. But hey, **snow is really pretty**."

"Be prepared for cold and wind. Though it's the Windy City, Chicago has nothing on North Campus, wind-wise—and December, January, February, and parts of March are frigid. Buffalo is **known for its snow**, but the reputation is not wholly deserved. The city itself actually receives less snow than both Rochester and Syracuse (the perennial upstate New York snow champion). The majority of the snow around Buffalo hits the south towns, not North Buffalo or Amherst."

"The truth is that **we're all in denial**. In every other city that braves the same sorts of arctic temperatures, they pay attention to wind chills. Here, we'd rather be wearing our Tevas in case the sun comes out."

"You can bring clothes for summer, but you probably won't need them until spring break. **It's ridiculously cold here**, and it doesn't let up until around the last day of classes."

"For the most part, the weather is decent up until winter break, but by the time you come back for spring semester, the **temperatures are in the single digits**, and the snow keeps falling until finals week. The best thing to do is just layer up and wear lots of hats, gloves, and scarves."

The College Prowler Take On...
Weather

Unless you live in a cave, you've probably seen this image on the Weather Channel: out-of-town correspondent reports on a Buffalo blizzard from just outside the city (she can't get in because of the driving ban). She's barely visible through sheets of snow. Maybe her hat blows off and disappears into the maelstrom. Buffalo's lake effect "snow events" are legendary—12 feet of snow fell in one week in 2001, and a drive-time storm in 2000 left thousands stranded in their cars. But blizzards are fun for most students who sit in their cozy dorms or houses and celebrate with beer and hot chocolate, emerging the next morning to explore the new landscape.

The thing students loathe about Buffalo winters is that they last forever. Buffalo school kids get used to wearing parkas over their ghost costumes on Halloween, and the cold, wind, and snow don't stop until they search for Easter baskets in April. Many students get to know winter's fun side. Nearly 3,000 of them join Schussmeisters, a ski club with nightly buses to gorgeous ski resorts an hour south of the city. But a majority of students hate the winter, especially the bleakest days, when the day never quite wrestles free from the night. Spring is short and rainy in Buffalo. Summers are magnificent; there is more sun and less rain than any city in the Northeast. Longtime Buffalo residents wax poetic about harsh winters and how the four seasons benefit the soul. But Buffalo's winter is like a high school summer job. It seems like fun looking back, but when you're in the middle of it, you just want it to be over so you can go to the beach.

D-

The College Prowler® Grade on

Weather: D-

A high Weather grade designates that temperatures are mild and rarely reach extremes, that the campus tends to be sunny rather than rainy, and that weather is fairly consistent rather than unpredictable.

Report Card Summary

Grade	Category	Grade	Category
B	ACADEMICS	B	GUYS
B+	LOCAL ATMOSPHERE	B+	GIRLS
C	SAFETY & SECURITY	B-	ATHLETICS
A	COMPUTERS	A	NIGHTLIFE
A-	FACILITIES	C-	GREEK LIFE
B-	CAMPUS DINING	B+	DRUG SCENE
A-	OFF-CAMPUS DINING	B	CAMPUS STRICTNESS
B-	CAMPUS HOUSING	C	PARKING
A-	OFF-CAMPUS HOUSING	A-	TRANSPORTATION
B-	DIVERSITY	D-	WEATHER

Overall Experience

Students Speak Out On... Overall Experience

"I have never wished I was anywhere else. Even with so many people here at this school, you will have a chance to be somebody big. You will have the best time of your life."

"Buffalo wasn't my first choice. I came here because the price was right. But now that I'm here, I can't imagine being anywhere else. I'm as happy as can be. But then again, I also know people who aren't nearly as happy as I am. The experience is **what you make of it**. If you just sit around all day, that's what you'll get out of UB."

"I could not have had a more fulfilling college career. I switched my major twice, and you can do that here with **so many programs to choose from**. I have fallen in love with the area, the people, and the culture of Buffalo. It's vibrant and alive, and I have loved every minute of going to school here. This place is full of idiosyncrasies, but those are what make it great. You will not regret the choice to come to UB."

"I love UB—good people and good parties. **You can't beat the price** if you live in-state, because the education you get for most of the majors is excellent. Most of the professors have won awards and written their own books."

"My overall experience at UB **so far has been negative**. Oftentimes, I do wish I was somewhere else, and I can't imagine what I was thinking when I decided to go to school in Buffalo. But the people here are good, and I've met many lifelong friends. If it were up to me, I would transplant all of my experiences and all of my friends about a thousand miles south. Then I would be happy."

"I have loved every second that I have been at UB. I've had some of the best laughs as my friends and I slipped and sloshed our way home from a party in the middle of winter, with our arms linked, wearing our high heels and freezing our well-dressed tails off. I've had some of the most interesting professors—and I've had some horrible professors (who taught me how to handle myself when insane people are in authority). I got involved in organizations that exposed me to people of different backgrounds and gave me fresh takes on the world. My experience at UB has gone **beyond what I expected from university life**."

"**UB is a really great school**. It's a fantastic mix of old-school institutionalism and forward-thinking programming. I'm glad that I'll be able to call UB my alma mater, and when I actually find the time to graduate, I'll feel happy to have spent the best six years of my life at UB."

"The honors program **allowed me to get tight with a small group** of kids when I was a freshman, despite the enormity of the campus. After I found that core group of friends, I made so many others in my department and at my two University jobs. As a senior, it's hard to walk the length of one campus building without waving hello to someone or giving a high-five."

"I really enjoy being at this University. It is a great place, and **I love the city of Buffalo**. There is so much history, and it has so much potential (even if the city is in trouble now). UB is a major player in western New York life, and it has the potential to make even more of a difference for the city of Buffalo than it already has."

"I have **enjoyed UB to the fullest extent**. I'm happy to be here, and I wouldn't trade it for anywhere else."

"There are opportunities to **do just about anything** you want, and the size of the school allows you to try lots of new things. If you don't like it at UB, there's a good chance you should have tried to make more of it, and you have only yourself to blame."

"My overall experience at UB has been terrific. UB offers **unlimited opportunity in most everything** you can be interested in. Academically, I have developed my interests and discovered new interests. Away from academics, UB has offered many enriching experiences, as well."

The College Prowler Take On...
Overall Experience

From the overwhelmingly diverse campus culture to the odd architecture, UB takes some getting used to. But nearly all students say they've gotten a lot out of their four (or five, or six) years here, and many simply love the place. There are some institutional problems that get people down: administrative hassles, bland campus food, and rotten parking. The decentralized campus can lead to a diminished feeling of community. And the weather is a challenge to the spirit. But UB's modern facilities and world-class computer network get high marks, and most UB students grow to appreciate the great academics, the friendly people, and Buffalo's high quality of life.

UB has a great college experience waiting, but instead of gently offering it to you, it challenges you to "come and get it." If you're not intimidated by the diversity and the sprawling campus and if you get involved, you'll have an eclectic and inspirational experience. Students say UB is no utopia, but it's a lot of fun. And when it's over, nearly everyone remembers it fondly.

The Inside Scoop

The Lowdown On...
The Inside Scoop

UB Slang:

Know the slang, know the school. The following is a list of things you really need to know before coming to UB.

The Base – Third Base bar on Main Street, the "last stop before going home."

The Big White Box – The large concrete Center for the Arts on North Campus.

Blue Bird – The bus service that shuttles students between campuses, the nickname lives, even though the buses are no longer blue.

Buff State – An entirely separate school in Buffalo, located on the West Side; a few students every year actually apply to the wrong school, maybe because Buff State's address and academic information appeared under UB's entry in the 2000 *Fiske Guide to Colleges.*

CFA – The Center for the Arts.

Cheektavegas – Cheektowaga, Buffalo's predominantly Polish suburb—home of the airport, the Galleria Mall, Buffalo's best Polish restaurants, several tacky '60s-era strip plazas, and a proposed casino.

Chippewa – A club and bar district downtown.

CIT – The Office of Computing and Information Technology.

Cybrary – A computer lab in a campus library.

Drunk Bus – The early-hours intercampus shuttle that runs students from North Campus dorms and apartments to the Heights bars.

Elmwood Village – A beautiful West Side neighborhood full of Victorian homes, independent shops, and great restaurants; particularly popular with professors and grad students

EOP – The Equal Opportunity Program for economically disadvantaged students.

Governerds – Residents of Governors, often first-year athletes or honors students.

The Heights – The run-down but loved neighborhood adjacent to South Campus where thousands of UB students live.

Kung Fu Tai Chi Guy – An old man who sits at various locations around campus holding a sign that says "LEARN KUNG FU TAI CHI."

The Lake – Not Lake Erie, but manmade Lake LaSalle on North Campus.

Legoland – Another name for the unusual-looking Ellicott Complex.

NSC – A big building on North Campus that houses most of the science departments and several huge lecture halls.

The Ralph – Ralph Wilson Stadium, home of the Bills, about 25 minutes from campus in Orchard Park.

Smellicott – The Ellicott Complex (particularly Wilkeson and Spaulding Quads, the all-freshman section).

The Spine – A mile-long cluster of huge buildings on North Campus where most of the academic departments are housed.

SU – The Student Union; the gateway to the Spine from the main bus loop.

The UGL – Undergraduate Library, which is louder than many cafeterias.

Wide Right – All Buffalonians flinch at this phrase, which refers to Scott Norwood's missed field goal as time expired on the Bills' 20–19 loss to the Giants in Super Bowl XXV.

Things I Wish I Knew Before Coming to UB

- You don't need to decide what you want to study right away.
- It's tough to get by without a car.
- Don't buy "college clothes" because most people dress down.
- It's not easy to make friends in big classes.
- 8 a.m. classes are nearly impossible to get up for.

Tips to Succeed at UB

- If you're from the Buffalo area, live on campus your freshman year instead of living at home.
- Don't hook up too much in your first couple of months as a freshman.
- Visit professors during their office hours; even popular professors love to talk to students.
- Get off campus and immerse yourself in Buffalo's culture as much as you can.
- Study in Lockwood Library instead of the UGL or at your dorms.
- If you get stuck in a big lecture hall, introduce yourself to the professor in the second week and sit in the front of the class.
- Try to get into the Honors Program; you can get early registration.

(Tips to Succeed at UB, continued)

- Find a place you can park illegally without getting caught.
- Take as many small classes as possible.
- Join a sport, club, or student government.
- Don't get depressed by the sterility of the campus.
- Learn which professors are good and which ones aren't.
- Figure out how to navigate the bridges and indoor tunnels.

UB Urban Legends

- North Campus was originally supposed to be built on the waterfront.
- The campus was designed without central gathering spaces in response to UB's violent Vietnam War protests.
- Former President Greiner complained about the bronze buffalo in front of Alumni Arena because its rear end faced his office.
- The Ellicott Complex was modeled after a Chinese prison.
- The campus is sinking slowly because it was built on a marsh.

School Spirit

In terms of school spirit, UB is far less than the sum of its parts. The University is made of many small communities—academic units, sports, clubs, and social groups, but these communities don't add up to a cohesive whole. Most students are happy in their corner of the University, but can muster only lukewarm spirit for the larger institution. Students credit all the fun parts of their years in Buffalo (parties, friendships, achievements) to their communities within UB, while they blame the institution as a whole for all the depressing parts (huge classes, monolithic architecture, parking, and the weather).

Since the 1990s, the administration has poured money into the football and basketball programs, hoping that their success would unite the campus. With the exception of basketball, this effort has yet to pay off (if anything, the football team's problems have increased student apathy). Nevertheless, there's a core of students at UB who love the school, despite its flaws. Many students grow to love Buffalo, as well.

Traditions

Cultural Nights

Each international student association on campus (e.g., the Indian Student Association) holds a major ethnic festival or cultural night at least once a year on campus. Often, these events are held at the 2,000-seat Mainstage Theater at the CFA and feature ethnic dancing, music, and food.

Fall Fest and Spring Fest

Each fall and spring, the Student Association brings big-time bands to UB for a free concert that's often attended by over 10,000 students. Past shows include Outkast and Dave Matthews Band. If it's nice out, they'll have the concert at Baird Point—nothing beats a free concert with those giant pillars and the sun setting over the lake as a backdrop. Lots of students have big parties over Fall Fest and Spring Fest weekends.

Oozfest

In the spring, everybody who's anybody on campus plays in Oozfest, an infamous mud volleyball tournament. There are special courts off in the corner of campus that are reserved for Oozfest each year, and sometimes students go early just to roll around in the mud pit.

Opening Day

Though the football team hasn't had a winning season since the mid-'90s, UB fans always start each season with high hopes. Usually over 25,000 fans come out for the first home game. UB Stadium on North Campus is a beautiful facility, and the energy is electric—at least, until they lose.

Finding a Job or Internship

The Lowdown On... Finding a Job or Internship

In preparing for a job search, students typically fall into one of two extremes. Some students shape their entire college experience towards getting that first job, like that kid who's dreamed of being an FBI agent since the early '90s when he or she stayed up on Sunday night to watch the *X-Files*. On the other side of the coin, most students are shell-shocked when they realize sometime during senior year that they won't be at UB forever. However, it's possible to find a middle ground—a way to experience UB on your own terms and still be ready to get a good job when your time's up. The key is to take the classes you want, have the summer experiences you want, and join the clubs you want. At the same time, get to know as many of your professors as you can; take advantage of academic opportunities, including research; and visit the Office of Career Services early and regularly. You won't sell your soul to the FBI (or to Silicon Valley, Wall Street, or Capitol Hill), but you'll be ready to get jobs there when you graduate.

Advice

Ironically, the people who will be most useful to you in the job search are also people who don't have real jobs: professors. While most students think they're most useful for recommendations, they can also get you involved in the study groups and research projects that make your resumé shine.

At UB, the Office of Career Services is also an invaluable resource, and not just late in your college career when the job search is thrust upon you. Visit the office right away in your freshman year. It's far too small for a school of UB's size, so it's tough to make an appointment, but do it anyway. You'll probably like your counselor. (They seem like they're trained to be likeable at a friendliness boot camp.) Everyone's warm and smiley, and the offices are painted in happy colors like your old pediatrician's waiting room.

After your first visit, go back to the same counselor once every semester. At the very least, they'll get you thinking about the inevitable job search, and you'll have a friendly face in Capen Hall who knows your name.

Firms that Most Frequently Hire Graduates

Bank of America, Boeing, Citigroup, Comp USA, M&T, Deloitte & Touche, DuPont, Eckerd, ECMC, Enterprise, Ernst & Young, Exxon, FedEx, Fisher-Price, Fleet Bank, General Dynamics, General Electric, General Motors, GEICO, HSBC, IBM, Kaleida, Kenmore Mercy, KPMG, Microsoft, Morgan Stanley, Niagara Mohawk, Northrop Grummen, Paychex, Pepsi, Pfizer, Praxair, Price Waterhouse, Rite Aid, Roswell Park Cancer Inst., Stantec Consulting, Time Warner, Toshiba, UPS, Verizon, WKBW-TV, Xerox

Career Center Resources & Services

- Career counseling
- Career resource library
- Computerized testing center (GRE, GMAT, PRAXIS, TOEFL)
- Job and internship listings
- Job fairs and workshops
- Mentoring
- On-campus employment opportunities
- On-campus interviewing
- "Quick Question Counseling" walk-in service
- Resumé referrals
- UBE 202: A three-credit course designed to help you find a major or career

Grads Who Enter the Job Market Within

6 Months: N/A

1 Year: 73%

Alumni

The Lowdown On...
Alumni

Web Site:
www.alumni.buffalo.edu

Office:
Office of Alumni Relations
109 Allen Hall
3435 Main St.
Buffalo, NY 14214
ub-alumni@buffalo.edu
1-800-BUILD-UB

Services Available:
Access to UB libraries
Alumni locator
Career-related events and networking opportunities
Chapter events in major U.S. cities and foreign countries
Discounts on UB-related items, such as Kaplan courses and Bulls tickets
Relocation assistance (from or to Buffalo)
Special insurance and credit card offers
Special travel offers

Major Alumni Events

While UB has over 175,000 living alumni, they're not as visibly involved in campus life as at many other schools. UB's alumni giving rate is a relatively low eight percent. However, alumni do come back to town for the Homecoming football game and for the various class reunions. The Office of Alumni Relations also organizes six alumni trips each year, including a steamboat trip on the Mississippi and a week in a Tuscan villa.

Alumni Publications

UB's Alumni Association publishes *UB Today*, a glossy quarterly magazine. *UB Today* is available online at *www.buffalo.edu/UBT.*

Did You Know?

It's appropriate that the Office of Alumni Relations is located on South Campus, because North Campus didn't open until 1973. Many living UB alumni have never set foot on it.

Famous UB Alumni

Millard S. Drexler (Class of '66) – President and CEO of Gap

Ronald A. Silver (Class of '67) – Tony Award-winning actor and director

Wolf Blitzer (Class of '70) – CNN anchor and Washington Bureau Chief

Tom Toles (Class of '73) – Pulitzer Prize-winning cartoonist for the *Washington Post*

Harvey Weinstein (Class of '73) – CEO of Miramax Films

Ellen Shulman Baker (Class of '74) – Astronaut and missions specialist aboard Atlantis

Howard Kurtz (Class of '74) – Host of CNN's *Reliable Sources*

Brad Grey (Class of '79) – CEO of Brillstein-Grey Entertainment, which produces the *Sopranos*

Student Organizations

A full list of student organizations at UB is available from the Student Association Web site, located at *www.sa.buffalo.edu*.

Academic

Association for Computing Machinery
AIESEC
Alpha Epsilon Delta
Anthropology SA
Art Historical Association
Association of Pre-Med Students
Communication Undergraduate SA
Environmental Network
French Club
Geography SA
Geology SA
Medical Biotechnology SA
Minorities in Health Related Professions
Minority Management

(Academic Organizations, continued)

Minority Nursing SA
Nursing Student Organization
Poltical Science SA
Pre-law Society
Pre Dental
Student Affiliates of the American Chemical Society
Student Association of Speech & Hearing
Student Visual Arts Organization
Undergraduate Psychology SA

Engineering

American Institute of Aeronautics & Astronautics
American Institute of Chemical Engineers
American Society of Civil Engineers
American Society of Mechanical Engineers
Institute of Electrical & Electronic Engineering
Institute of Industrial Engineers
National Society of Black Engineers
UB Robotics
Society of Automotive Engineers
Society of Hispanic Professional Engineers
Society of Women Engineers
Solex Club

International

African SA
Bangladeshi SA
Caribbean SA
Chinese SA
Filipino-American SA
Haitian SA
Indian SA
Indonesian SA (Permias)

(International Organizations, continued)

Japanese SA
Korean SA
Latin American SA
Malaysian SA
Organization of Arab Students
Pakistani SA
Polish SA
Taiwanese SA
Turkish SA
Ukranian SA
Vietnamese SA

People of Color

Asian American Srudent Union
Black Student Union (BSU)
NAACP
Native American Peoples Alliance
PODER: Latinos Unidos

Special Interest, Service, and Hobby

Baha'i SA
Ballroom Dance
Bible Talk
Bhangra
Circle K
Club Dance Dance Revolution
College Democrats
College Republicans
Combined Martial Arts
Community Action Corps (CAC)
EOP SA
Gospel Choir

(Special Interest Organizations, continued)

Hip Hop SA

Impulse Dance Force

Inter-Varsity Christian Fellowship

Jewish Student Union

Korean Student Union

Leaders Student Association

LGBTA

Mock Trial

Muslim SA

Outdoor Adventure Club

Pagan SA

Sankofa! Dance Troupe

SARPA

SMASH Club

Step Troupe

UB Anime

UB Dazzlers

UB Veterans Fraternity

The Best & Worst

The Ten **BEST** Things About UB

1. Academics that range from good to extraordinary
2. The genuine, unpretentious, laid-back friendliness of everyone you meet
3. Living in a sophisticated town with some of the best art and architecture in the world
4. 4 a.m. club/bar closing time
5. Great food, from greasy wings to classy martini bars
6. Paying for your off-campus apartment with coins you find in the couch cushions
7. Schussmeisters nights at Holiday Valley with 3,000 of your closest friends
8. 20 minutes from one of the world's natural wonders (itself two minutes from 19-and-over bars)

9. Sharing the excitement of a Bills victory with two-thirds of the campus

10. Getting a potentially world-class education for chump change

The Ten WORST Things About UB

1. Parking in Siberia

2. North Campus's dreary isolation and Stalinist architecture (to continue the Russia metaphor)

3. The football team reaching the top—of ESPN's "Bottom 10"

4. Finding things in the campus food

5. Writing your student ID on a test instead of your name

6. Guys who drive tricked-out Hondas and act like they never graduated from high school

7. Getting lost in Ellicott after living there for three years

8. Ten minutes to class, and it's on South Campus

9. The debate over whether to call that carbonated drink "pop" or "soda"

10. Blizzards!

Visiting

The Lowdown On... Visiting

Hotel Information:

While Amherst's cookie-cutter suburban chains are more convenient to campus, I recommend staying downtown and touring the city on your visit. Buffalo's shops, restaurants, and cultural attractions are important to the UB experience. A tour of UB would be incomplete without them. Go to the Buffalo Niagara region tourism site (*www.visitbuffaloniagara.com*) to learn more about touring the Queen City.

The Visit UB program is located on North Campus. Because some first-year students live on South Campus; however, I have provided distances to both campuses.

→

Amherst:

Buffalo Niagara Marriott

1340 Millersport Hwy.
Amherst, NY 14221

(716) 689-6900

http://marriott.com/property/propertypage/bufny

Distance from North Campus: Less than a mile

Distance from South Campus: 2.5 miles

Price Range: $76–$150

Courtyard by Marriott

4100 Sheridan Dr.
Amherst, NY 14221

(716) 626-2300

www.courtyard.com

Distance from North Campus: 1.5 miles

Distance from South Campus: 3 miles

Price Range: $69–$219

Hampton Inn

10 Flint Rd.
Amherst, NY 14226

(716) 689-4414

www.hamptoninnbuffaloamherst.com

Distance from North Campus: Across the street from campus

Distance from South Campus: 3 miles

Price Range: $69–$179

Holiday Inn Buffalo/Amherst

1881 Niagara Falls Blvd.
Amherst, NY 14228

(716) 691-8181

www.hibuffaloamherst.com

Distance from North Campus: 2 miles

Distance from South Campus: 4 miles

Price Range: $59–$109

Motel 6

4400 Maple Rd.
Amherst, NY 14226

(716) 834-2231

Distance from North Campus: 1 mile

Distance from South Campus: 3 miles

Price Range: $35–$50

Red Roof Inn

42 Flint Rd.
Amherst, NY 14226

(716) 689-7474

www.redroof.com

Distance from North Campus: Across the street from campus

Distance from South Campus: 3 miles

Price Range: $50–$125

Travelodge/University District

3612 Main St.
Buffalo, NY 14226

(716) 837-3344

Distance from North Campus: 3 miles

Distance from South Campus: Across the street from campus

Price Range: $51–$75

University Inn & Conference Center

2401 N Forest Rd.
Amherst, NY 14226

(716) 636-7500

www.universityinn.com

Distance from North Campus: Across the street from campus

Distance from South Campus: 5 miles

Price Range: $76–$150

Downtown Buffalo:

Adam's Mark Hotel

120 Church St.
Buffalo, NY 14202

(716) 845-5100

www.adamsmark.com/buffalo

Distance from North Campus: 15 miles

Distance from South Campus: 7 miles

Price Range: $78–$189

Best Western Inn on the Avenue

510 Delaware Ave.
Buffalo, NY 14202

(716) 886-8333

www.innontheavenue.com

Distance from North Campus: 13 miles

Distance from South Campus: 5 miles

Price Range: $76–$125

Doubletree Club Hotel

125 High St.
Buffalo, NY 14203

(716) 845-0112

www.doubletree.com

Distance from North Campus: 12 miles

Distance from South Campus: 5 miles

Price Range: $79–$109

Hampton Inn & Suites

220 Delaware Ave.
Buffalo, NY 14202

(716) 855-2223

www.hamptoninnbuffalo.com

Distance from North Campus: 13 miles

Distance from South Campus: 6 miles

Price Range: $80–$189

Holiday Inn Downtown

620 Delaware Ave.
Buffalo, NY 14202

(716) 886-2121

www.hibuffalodowntown.com

Distance from North Campus: 13 miles

Distance from South Campus: 5 miles

Price Range: $76–$125

Hyatt Regency Buffalo

2 Fountain Plaza
Buffalo, NY 14202

(716) 856-1234

www.buffalo.hyatt.com

Distance from North Campus: 13 miles

Distance from South Campus: 6 miles

Price Range: $76–$200

Lenox Hotel & Suites

140 North St.
Buffalo, NY 14201

(716) 884-1700

www.lenoxhotelandsuites.com

Distance from North Campus: 12.5 miles

Distance from South Campus: 5 miles

Price Range: $51–$150

The Mansion on Delaware Avenue

414 Delaware Ave.
Buffalo, NY 14202

(716) 886-3300

www.mansionondelaware.com

Distance from North Campus: 13 miles

Distance from South Campus: 5 miles

Price Range: $126–$150

Take a Campus Virtual Tour

www.buffalo.edu/tour

To Schedule a Group Information Session or Interview

A program called "Visit UB" schedules information sessions and campus tours with enthusiastic students called "UB Stars." To reserve a spot with Visit UB, and you must do so two weeks in advance, call 1-888-UB-ADMIT, E-mail ub-admissions@buffalo.edu, or register online at *www.buffalo.edu/vub.*

Campus Tours

Campus tours are offered Monday through Friday at 1 p.m. The program begins with an information session in Capen Hall and ends with a lengthy campus tour. Pack your walking shoes.

Overnight Visits

UB doesn't have a formal overnight visit program. But if you're from New York State, it's more than likely that somebody from your high school went to UB, so talk to your guidance counselor.

Directions To North Campus

Driving from the North (Toronto)

- Take the Queen Elizabeth Way south to the Peace Bridge.
- Follow Interstate 190 North to Interstate 290 East.
- Follow Interstate 290 East to Interstate 990 (Exit 4).
- From Interstate 990, take Exit 1 (Univ at Buffalo North Campus).
- Make a left at the first light (Rensch Road).
- Make a left at the stop sign onto Hadley Road.
- Make a right at the stop sign onto White Road.
- Make a right and proceed into the visitors' parking lot (if after 3 p.m. or on a weekend, you may park in any lot).

Driving from the South and West (Pittsburgh and Cleveland)

- Follow Interstate 90 West to Exit 50 (Interstate 290 West/ Niagara Falls).
- Follow Interstate 290 West to Exit 5B (Millersport Highway).
- After the light, take the exit for Flint Entrance. Merge onto Audubon Parkway, and go straight at the light.
- After the road bends, make a right at the next light (Rensch Road).
- Make a left at the stop sign onto Hadley Road.
- Make a right at the stop sign onto White Road.
- Make a right and proceed into the visitors' parking lot (if after 3 p.m. or on a weekend, you may park in any lot).

Driving from the East (Boston, Upstate New York, Albany and New York City)

- From Long Island, New York City, and the Hudson Valley, take Interstate 87 North to Interstate 90 West (NYS Thruway) near Albany.
- From Albany and all upstate New York locations, follow Interstate 90 West to Exit 50 (Interstate 290 West/Niagara Falls).
- Follow Interstate 290 West to Exit 5B (Millersport Highway).
- After the first light, take the exit for Flint Entrance. Merge onto Audubon Parkway, and go straight at the light.
- After the road bends, make a right at the next light (Rensch Road).
- Make a left at the stop sign onto Hadley Road.
- Make a right at the stop sign onto White Road.
- Make a right and proceed into the visitors' parking lot (if after 3 p.m. or on a weekend, you may park in any lot).

Words to Know

Academic Probation – A suspension imposed on a student if he or she fails to keep up with the school's minimum academic requirements. Those unable to improve their grades after receiving this warning can face dismissal.

Beer Pong/Beirut – A drinking game involving cups of beer arranged in a pyramid shape on each side of a table. The goal is to get a ping pong ball into one of the opponent's cups by throwing the ball or hitting it with a paddle. If the ball lands in a cup, the opponent is required to drink the beer.

Bid – An invitation from a fraternity or sorority to 'pledge' (join) that specific house.

Blue-Light Phone – Brightly-colored phone posts with a blue light bulb on top. These phones exist for security purposes and are located at various outside locations around most campuses. In an emergency, a student can pick up one of these phones (free of charge) to connect with campus police or a security escort.

Campus Police – Police who are specifically assigned to a given institution. Campus police are typically not regular city officers; they are employed by the university in a full-time capacity.

Club Sports – A level of sports that falls somewhere between varsity and intramural. If a student is unable to commit to a varsity team but has a lot of passion for athletics, a club sport could be a better, less intense option. Even less demanding, intramural (IM) sports often involve no traveling and considerably less time.

Cocaine – An illegal drug. Also known as "coke" or "blow," cocaine often resembles a white crystalline or powdery substance. It is highly addictive and dangerous.

Common Application – An application with which students can apply to multiple schools.

Course Registration – The period of official class selection for the upcoming quarter or semester. Prior to registration, it is best to prepare several back-up courses in case a particular class becomes full. If a course is full, students can place themselves on the waitlist, although this still does not guarantee entry.

Division Athletics – Athletic classifications range from Division I to Division III. Division IA is the most competitive, while Division III is considered to be the least competitive.

Dorm – A dorm (or dormitory) is an on-campus housing facility. Dorms can provide a range of options from suite-style rooms to more communal options that include shared bathrooms. Most first-year students live in dorms. Some upperclassmen who wish to stay on campus also choose this option.

Early Action – An application option with which a student can apply to a school and receive an early acceptance response without a binding commitment. This system is becoming less and less available.

Early Decision – An application option that students should use only if they are certain they plan to attend the school in question. If a student applies using the early decision option and is admitted, he or she is required and bound to attend that university. Admission rates are usually higher among students who apply through early decision, as the student is clearly indicating that the school is his or her first choice.

Ecstasy – An illegal drug. Also known as "E" or "X," ecstasy looks like a pill and most resembles an aspirin. Considered a party drug, ecstasy is very dangerous and can be deadly.

Ethernet – An extremely fast Internet connection available in most university-owned residence halls. To use an Ethernet connection properly, a student will need a network card and cable for his or her computer.

Fake ID – A counterfeit identification card that contains false information. Most commonly, students get fake IDs with altered birthdates so that they appear to be older than 21 (and therefore of legal drinking age). Even though it is illegal, many college students have fake IDs in hopes of purchasing alcohol or getting into bars.

Frosh – Slang for "freshman" or "freshmen."

Hazing – Initiation rituals administered by some fraternities or sororities as part of the pledging process. Many universities have outlawed hazing due to its degrading, and sometimes dangerous, nature.

Intramurals (IMs) – A popular, and usually free, sport league in which students create teams and compete against one another. These sports vary in competitiveness and can include a range of activities—everything from billiards to water polo. IM sports are a great way to meet people with similar interests.

Keg – Officially called a half-barrel, a keg contains roughly 200 12-ounce servings of beer.

LSD – An illegal drug, also known as acid, this hallucinogenic drug most commonly resembles a tab of paper.

Marijuana – An illegal drug, also known as weed or pot; along with alcohol, marijuana is one of the most commonly-found drugs on campuses across the country.

Major –The focal point of a student's college studies; a specific topic that is studied for a degree. Examples of majors include physics, English, history, computer science, economics, business, and music. Many students decide on a specific major before arriving on campus, while others are simply "undecided" until declaring a major. Those who are extremely interested in two areas can also choose to double major.

Meal Block – The equivalent of one meal. Students on a meal plan usually receive a fixed number of meals per week. Each meal, or "block," can be redeemed at the school's dining facilities in place of cash. Often, a student's weekly allotment of meal blocks will be forfeited if not used.

Minor – An additional focal point in a student's education. Often serving as a complement or addition to a student's main area of focus, a minor has fewer requirements and prerequisites to fulfill than a major. Minors are not required for graduation from most schools; however some students who want to explore many different interests choose to pursue both a major and a minor.

Mushrooms – An illegal drug. Also known as "'shrooms," this drug resembles regular mushrooms but is extremely hallucinogenic.

Off-Campus Housing – Housing from a particular landlord or rental group that is not affiliated with the university. Depending on the college, off-campus housing can range from extremely popular to non-existent. Students who choose to live off campus are typically given more freedom, but they also have to deal with possible subletting scenarios, furniture, bills, and other issues. In addition to these factors, rental prices and distance often affect a student's decision to move off campus.

Office Hours – Time that teachers set aside for students who have questions about coursework. Office hours are a good forum for students to go over any problems and to show interest in the subject material.

Pledging – The early phase of joining a fraternity or sorority, pledging takes place after a student has gone through rush and received a bid. Pledging usually lasts between one and two semesters. Once the pledging period is complete and a particular student has done everything that is required to become a member, that student is considered a brother or sister. If a fraternity or a sorority would decide to "haze" a group of students, this initiation would take place during the pledging period.

Private Institution – A school that does not use tax revenue to subsidize education costs. Private schools typically cost more than public schools and are usually smaller.

Prof – Slang for "professor."

Public Institution – A school that uses tax revenue to subsidize education costs. Public schools are often a good value for in-state residents and tend to be larger than most private colleges.

Quarter System (or Trimester System) – A type of academic calendar system. In this setup, students take classes for three academic periods. The first quarter usually starts in late September or early October and concludes right before Christmas. The second quarter usually starts around early to mid–January and finishes up around March or April. The last academic quarter, or "third quarter," usually starts in late March or early April and finishes up in late May or Mid-June. The fourth quarter is summer. The major difference between the quarter system and semester system is that students take more, less comprehensive courses under the quarter calendar.

RA (Resident Assistant) – A student leader who is assigned to a particular floor in a dormitory in order to help to the other students who live there. An RA's duties include ensuring student safety and providing assistance wherever possible.

Recitation – An extension of a specific course; a review session. Some classes, particularly large lectures, are supplemented with mandatory recitation sessions that provide a relatively personal class setting.

Rolling Admissions – A form of admissions. Most commonly found at public institutions, schools with this type of policy continue to accept students throughout the year until their class sizes are met. For example, some schools begin accepting students as early as December and will continue to do so until April or May.

Room and Board – This figure is typically the combined cost of a university-owned room and a meal plan.

Room Draw/Housing Lottery – A common way to pick on-campus room assignments for the following year. If a student decides to remain in university-owned housing, he or she is assigned a unique number that, along with seniority, is used to determine his or her housing for the next year.

Rush – The period in which students can meet the brothers and sisters of a particular chapter and find out if a given fraternity or sorority is right for them. Rushing a fraternity or a sorority is not a requirement at any school. The goal of rush is to give students who are serious about pledging a feel for what to expect.

Semester System – The most common type of academic calendar system at college campuses. This setup typically includes two semesters in a given school year. The fall semester starts around the end of August or early September and concludes before winter vacation. The spring semester usually starts in mid-January and ends in late April or May.

Student Center/Rec Center/Student Union – A common area on campus that often contains study areas, recreation facilities, and eateries. This building is often a good place to meet up with fellow students; depending on the school, the student center can have a huge role or a non-existent role in campus life.

Student ID – A university-issued photo ID that serves as a student's key to school-related functions. Some schools require students to show these cards in order to get into dorms, libraries, cafeterias, and other facilities. In addition to storing meal plan information, in some cases, a student ID can actually work as a debit card and allow students to purchase things from bookstores or local shops.

Suite – A type of dorm room. Unlike dorms that feature communal bathrooms shared by the entire floor, suites offer bathrooms shared only among the suite. Suite-style dorm rooms can house anywhere from two to ten students.

TA (Teacher's Assistant) – An undergraduate or grad student who helps in some manner with a specific course. In some cases, a TA will teach a class, assist a professor, grade assignments, or conduct office hours.

Undergraduate – A student in the process of studying for his or her bachelor's degree.

ABOUT THE AUTHOR

Wherever life takes me, I will always be a Buffalo boy. I love this old town, and I know it like the back of my hand. If there's one thing to say about Buffalo people, it's that they're honest—there's an old T-shirt around town that says, "Buffalo: City of No Illusions." I hope you find that I brought some of that honesty to this book. I've had fun showing you around.

I came to UB after earning an International Baccalaureate diploma at Buffalo's City Honors School. After four great years, I will graduate with an Advanced Honors degree in English and a minor in political science. Currently I serve as a managing editor and columnist for the *Spectrum*, UB's student newspaper. I'm a member of Phi Beta Kappa and a varsity athlete—I run cross-country in the fall and track and field in the spring.

When I say farewell to Buffalo, I plan to get involved in politics. I've had the good fortune of interning with the great Democratic senator Chuck Schumer in New York and the Democratic Senatorial Campaign Committee in Washington. Some day, I'd like to go to law school.

When my old track coach Dick Barry retired, he said, "Always remember two things: you never get anywhere alone, and you can never say thank you enough." In that spirit, I thank my mom and dad, my grandparents, my brother, Adam, Amanda, my girl, Mike Silverstein, Joel, Czyz, Lockett, McKenna, Strelick, and Wigton from the team, Flor, Coach Mitchell, Erin, George, Katie, Jeremy, Sam, Jen, Eric, Charity, Ben, Nick, Mike, Jim, John, Dena, Jeff, Lynn, Helene and Debbie from the paper, all of my coaches and teachers, including Mr. Anelli, Mr. Verso, Mr. Anthony, Mr. Fitz, Mr. Francescone, Mrs. Kiefer, Mr. Toy, Mr. LaChiusa, Dr. Battaglia, Dr. Hubbard, Dr. Daly, and Dr. Bono, everyone who filled out a survey, and not least of all, the good people of College Prowler for giving me this opportunity.

Ben Cady
bencady@collegeprowler.com

California Colleges

California dreamin'?

This book is a must have for you!

CALIFORNIA COLLEGES
7¼" X 10", 762 Pages Paperback
$29.95 Retail
1-59658-501-3

Stanford, UC Berkeley, Caltech—California is home to some of America's greatest institutes of higher learning. *California Colleges* gives the lowdown on 24 of the best, side by side, in one prodigious volume.

Schools of the South

Headin' down south? This book will help you find your way to the perfect school!

Schools of the South
7¼" X 10", 773 Pages Paperback
$29.95 Retail
1-59658-503-X

Southern pride is always strong. Whether it's across town or across state, many Southern students are devoted to their home sweet home. *Schools of the South* offers an honest student perspective on 36 universities available south of the Mason-Dixon.

Untangling the Ivy League

The ultimate book for everything Ivy!

UNTANGLING THE IVY LEAGUE
7¼" X 10", 567 Pages Paperback
$24.95 Retail
1-59658-500-5

Ivy League students, alumni, admissions officers, and other top insiders get together to tell it like it is. *Untangling the Ivy League* covers every aspect—from admissions and athletics to secret societies and urban legends—of the nation's eight oldest, wealthiest, and most competitive colleges and universities.

Pros and Cons

Still can't figure out if this is the right school for you? You've already read through this in-depth guide; why not list the pros and cons? It will really help with narrowing down your decision and determining whether or not this school is right for you.

Pros	Cons
....	....
....	....
....	....
....	....
....	....
....	....
....	....
....	....
....	....
....	....
....	....
....	....
....	....

COLLEGE PROWLER®

Pros and Cons

Still can't figure out if this is the right school for you? You've already read through this in-depth guide; why not list the pros and cons? It will really help with narrowing down your decision and determining whether or not this school is right for you.

Pros	Cons
....	....
....	....
....	....
....	....
....	....
....	....
....	....
....	....
....	....
....	....
....	....
....	....
....	....

College Prowler®

Notes

Notes

Notes

Notes

COLLEGE PROWLER®